RECONSIDERATIONS

LITERARY ESSAYS

RECONSIDERATIONS

LITERARY ESSAYS

by

E. E. KELLETT

CAMBRIDGE
AT THE UNIVERSITY PRESS
1928

CAMBRIDGE
UNIVERSITY PRESS

University Printing House, Cambridge CB2 8BS, United Kingdom

Published in the United States of America by Cambridge University Press, New York

Cambridge University Press is part of the University of Cambridge.

It furthers the University's mission by disseminating knowledge in the pursuit of education, learning and research at the highest international levels of excellence.

www.cambridge.org
Information on this title: www.cambridge.org/9781107426795

© Cambridge University Press 1928

First published 1928
First paperback edition 2014

A catalogue record for this publication is available from the British Library

ISBN 978-1-107-42679-5 Paperback

PREFACE

SOME of these essays have already appeared in the *London Mercury*, the *London Quarterly*, the *Contemporary*, and the *British Review*. To the editors of these publications I desire to make the usual acknowledgments. Nor must I omit to thank the staff of the University Press for the almost unfailing care and accuracy to which I owe the correction of many slips and of a few more serious errors.

The book will be found to contain some perhaps audacious traversings of opinions currently held or associated with distinguished names; as well as 'reconsiderations' of opinions I formerly held myself. Whatever may be thought of the views expressed, I may at any rate claim that modicum of indulgence which is due to sincerity. "Molesta veritas, sed obsequium multo molestius, quod peccatis indulgens praecipitem ferri sinit."

E. E. KELLETT

1928

CONTENTS

1 Chaucer and his Influence   *page* 1

2 Some Pitfalls in Shakespearean Criticism   32

3 Dramatic Silences   59

4 The Translation of the New Testament   77

5 Milton as Medievalist   105

6 Milton and Dante   128

7 Thomas Fuller   147

8 Pomfret's "Choice"   163

9 The "Ode to Duty"   182

10 Macaulay and the Authorised Version   200

11 Swinburne   219

12 Joseph Conrad   243

13 Critical Certainties   262

i

CHAUCER AND HIS INFLUENCE

FROM very early times till quite lately the custom was almost universal of beginning the history of English poetry with Chaucer. To his admirer and imitator Hoccleve he was "the *first* finder of our fair language," before whom there had been but clumsy manipulators of a barbarous tongue. To Daniel, two centuries later, he was the writer who had

> Won upon the mighty waste of days,
> Unto the immortal honour of our clime,
> That by his means came *first* adorned with bays.

Addison, a century later still, seems to have known as little of Chaucer as of what went before him; but he speaks to the same effect:

> Long had our dull forefathers slept supine,
> Nor felt the raptures of the tuneful Nine,
> Till Chaucer *first*, a merry bard, arose,
> And many a story told in rhyme and prose.

To Mason also—who attempted to imitate Chaucer —"Tityrus" was *first*.

The fancy persisted long. Precisely as to Milton and Hume the wars of our ancestors before the Norman Conquest seemed but like the quarrels of kites and crows, so to Dryden and Johnson, even to Coleridge and Wordsworth, the poems before Chaucer, if poems there were, were like the twitterings

of "smale foules" trying to "maken melodye."
To these critics Caedmon was but a name; Cynewulf not even a name; *Beowulf* and *Pearl* but slowly
mouldering manuscripts in the British Museum. The
whole of that great literature, which it has been the
work of the Early English Text Society to recover,
was then a sealed book, either entirely unknown, or
misinterpreted and despised. Apart from Chaucer
himself, probably "Mandeville," Langland, and
Gower were the only fourteenth-century writers
known even by name: and such references as are
made to them are astonishing in the ignorance they
reveal. All the rest, if not actually dead, were buried;
and Macaulay, writing in 1837, could say with truth
that "in the time of Henry the Eighth and Edward
the Sixth the Italian was the only modern language
that possessed anything that could be called a literature: all the valuable books then extant in all the
vernacular dialects of Europe would hardly have
filled a single shelf."

But even while Macaulay was writing these words,
a time was beginning which, in its lesser degree, was
not unlike the Renaissance of Greek learning centuries earlier. It was found out that there had been
great men before Agamemnon, and English poets
before Dan Chaucer. Thorkelin had already discovered and copied *Beowulf*; in 1843 Kemble published the poetry of the Vercelli codex, and revealed
to an astonished world the fact that a great poet,

whose name he disinterred from the riddling runes that hid it, had lived in England in the very time of the "kites and crows"; Thorpe reprinted Caedmon. A little later the monumental work of Christian Grein made easily accessible the whole mass of "Anglo-Saxon" poetry. Simultaneously, later works of high rank were unearthed. For example, the edition of *Gawain and the Green Knight*, by Sir Frederick Madden, showed to all who had eyes to see that here was a fourteenth-century poet, only slightly senior to Chaucer, and fully worthy of comparison with Chaucer himself. It was thus seen that for no less than seven hundred years before the "first" poet, there had existed an English literature, well repaying hard study, and, though perhaps uncouth at first sight, gaining immeasurably on closer acquaintance. The enthusiasm of the antiquary was reinforced by patriotism; for this literature, despite its visible obligations to Latin, might be regarded as essentially independent of foreign influence, and as almost exclusively the expression of the national spirit; whereas since Chaucer's time English poetry had been too largely a mere aspect of the great Catholic movement of Western civilisation. Doubtless there was some want of discrimination in the *furore* with which these ancient treasures were greeted. As at the Renaissance everything Greek was good, so now: every newly discovered region was an Eldorado; the poet of the *Christ* was solemnly compared with Milton, and *Bi Manna Craeftum* was dubbed a great poem. But the fact remains not only that the discovery, as a mere matter of antiquarianism, was important, but that English literature, apart from its invaluable gains from contact with French, Italian, and the Classics, was seen to be a plant of very vigorous growth, and that much of very high merit was recovered from the bank and shoal of time. Seeing by how narrow a chance these ancient monuments had been rescued from destruction, the world wisely resolved to let them run no such risks again. Hence we are sorry to see certain scholars reverting to the ancient heresy, and in their eagerness to claim for Chaucer his just praise, arrogating to him more than really belongs to him, and tending to belittle the pre-Chaucerian poetry without the excuse of ignorance which could be pleaded by Daniel and Addison. It was perhaps natural that Professor Lounsbury, who had devoted no small part of his life to writing three huge volumes upon Chaucer, should magnify his office, and imitate less learned people by calling Chaucer the "earliest of the great English poets." Much is to be pardoned to the writers of monographs. But when so broad-minded a student of literature as Sir Arthur Quiller-Couch falls into the same error, it is time to protest. Chaucer has merits enough in actual fact to be able to dispense with praise which is not his due; for every fresh investigation into the history of our language and our poetry only increases our sense of debt to him. But English poetry is too great a structure to be the work of a single man, be that man a Shakespeare himself. Such a structure demands nothing less than the silent and steady co-operation of a whole people through many ages; and—to change the metaphor—no single genius, however great, is more than an officer in that army. "All are but parts of one stupendous whole," in which one part is often as indispensable as another. It cannot be too strongly asserted, first, that had Chaucer never been born, our literature would have taken a course very similar to the one it actually did take; and, secondly, that the influences represented by him, great and beneficent as on the whole they undoubtedly were, had yet their serious defects, which had to be supplied from other quarters. Fortunately, the English race was not so barren as to be unable to supply those other forces. Had English poetry *really* been dominated by Chaucer to the extent supposed, it would have been a vastly less vital and powerful organism than it has been. There were elements of immense value and importance in that school which Chaucer, to judge from the style of his own work, despised and tried to destroy. Nay, if comparisons are to be made—and to one like the present writer, who owes more delight to Chaucer than he can well express, these comparisons are specially odious—some of these elements were of higher value than any to be found in the school of which Chaucer was the leader; and all true lovers of poetry, while recognising to the full the many benefits he has conferred on his art, must ever rejoice that he did not succeed in his destructive work. In a word, he was far from "the earliest of English poets," and English poetry, where it has been most vital, has since his time often moved on lines independent of him and *more in consonance with the lines of his predecessors.* For these predecessors, being English, worked unconsciously in accord with the English spirit; and whenever, since their time, English poetry has been most thoroughly natural, it has unconsciously recurred to the spirit of Caedmon, Cynewulf, and the author of *Gawain.* To prove this statement fully would demand at least a volume; it must be the aim of a short paper like the present merely to illustrate it by a few detached hints.

The most obvious, if not actually the greatest, achievement of Chaucer, was the final and definitive substitution of the new form of versification for the old. Already, it would seem, alliterative verse had been displaced in the south of England; but it retained more or less vitality in the north; and, allowing for anticipations here and reversions there, we may fairly say that to Chaucer, and the school of which he is the chief representative, is due the destruction of this once dominant measure, and also —to a lesser degree—of the ballad-forms parodied in *Sir Thopas*. In their place, he did not introduce, but improved and all but perfected the octosyllabic couplet, and then, sighing for more worlds to conquer, developed the iambic pentameter, which before his time had only appeared furtively and as it were by accident in English verse. This measure, as the basis of the *Rhyme Royal* and of the *Riding Rhyme* or heroic couplet, he handed down to future generations to imitate and manipulate, but not to better. The service he did to literature in this respect it is impossible to overestimate: the flash of genius by which he saw the extraordinary adaptability of this metre to almost all conceivable poetical uses, marks him at once as a supreme artist in verse. What English literature would be without this metre is hard indeed to imagine. And not the least significant tribute to Chaucer's greatness is the fact that modern poets have returned to his use of it, and have shunned the form of it which was developed by the Augustan writers. As "perfected" by Waller, Dryden, and Pope, the metre is now worn out and dead. As a living form, as employed by Keats in *Endymion*, by Shelley in *Epipsychidion*, by Swinburne in *Tristram*, the metre is not that of Pope but that of the *Canterbury Tales*. Thus Chaucer, like Edward the Third, is the ancestor of two rival dynasties, the legitimate and the illegitimate. It is true that he allows himself certain licenses, natural in the experiments of a pioneer, which are now not permitted, or at any rate frequently used. Such are the truncated first foot,

> Twenty bokes clad in black and red,
> Twenty thousand freres in a route,

and the like; or the extra syllable so commonly found at the "caesura"—a freedom regular in the Elizabethans. But in his ease and lightness of scansion, and in his general treatment of the rhyming scheme, Chaucer has set the standard for to-day.

There is no need to mention here the many other metres which he tried, with great skill and ingenuity, at various times—the eight-line stanza of the *Monk's Tale*, for example, which was to give birth in the process of years to Spenser's immortal verse; or the many experiments like those in *Anelida and Arcite*, which, interesting as they are in themselves, are too elaborate to have given rise to more than a few imitations. Amid all these varieties, he preserved the beauty of his line; and it is undeniable that the iambic pentameter, in various combinations and in many forms, is to all intents and purposes the creation of Chaucer, who, moreover, not only created it, but brought it to perfection.

And yet, in those old metres which he despised, there was much which even his decasyllabic, at least in its rhyming form, could scarcely give. It is perfectly true that the *rum ram ruf* of the alliterative line, as Chaucer knew it and could not help knowing it, was loose and even licentious. In the fourteenth century, as used in *Piers the Plowman*, in *Gawain and the Green Knight*, in *William of Palerne* and a score of other poems, it bears every mark of having been a deliberate and somewhat ignorant *revival* of an old form; of having been a reaction against the tendencies of the day, and a purposed recurrence to what had been the tendencies of former times; and it had many of the defects of such revivals. For instance, whereas the metre of *Beowulf*, though easy and varied, had its precise and definite rules, and its limits beyond which it rarely or never strayed, the metre of *Piers the Plowman* apparently had none; it is an unweeded garden that too often runs to seed. Old English metres, as is well known, reduce themselves to five or six more or less rigidly defined types; and it is rarely indeed that a line, not obviously corrupt, fails to conform to one or other of these types. But he would be a bold man who would declare that he can see any type, or any number of types, to which the alliterative writers of the fourteenth century conformed or tried to conform. Hence Chaucer, as the apostle of law, may well have been right in revolting against this anarchy, nor can we be surprised that he did not recognise the true powers of the metre at its best; for the poems in which it was used at its best were not accessible to him. But in scholars of our time, to whom such poems *are* accessible, such a one-sided view is unpardonable; for we can see, as Chaucer could not, its capacities: and we can rejoice that even he, with all his influence, did not destroy it altogether, but that it lingered on, at least in the north, for a hundred years after his death. For we do not need to be told that, when used by a master who knows how to curb its laxities and restrain its exuberances, it has often a roll and a majesty which we seek in vain in the "ten-syllabled" couplet, and which indeed not even the Rhyme Royal always attains. The almost entire absence of rhyme, again, lends it some small degree of the dignity which we find in the blank verse of Milton; and even the alliteration, which occasionally palls, has at times for us to-day the full forceful value which, as far as we can guess, it had for its original hearers. Alliteration, indeed, seems to be an almost inevitable element in English poetry. Even when banished, it has a tendency to return. Spenser, while imitating Chaucer in so much else, imitated the balladists in his constant alliterations, and Swinburne, while restoring to us much of the ease of medieval metres, restored alliteration with it. There was, in fact, as Sir Israel Gollancz says, *a grandeur, a flexibility, and a vigour* in the metre of a Cynewulf which is ill compensated by the greater regularity and smoothness of the metres introduced by Chaucer. And all this, being *demanded* by the English nature, had to be recovered somehow; but it was not found in its old fullness till blank verse was invented—a measure of greater capacity than any of those used by Chaucer, and in many respects resembling the alliterative measure which he had helped to abolish.

And the same may be said, with a difference, of the shorter metres of Chaucer's time. There is a monotony, for example, in the octosyllabics of the *House of Fame*, which contrasts very unfavourably with the endless variety of the easy accentual system of the *Pearl*. Here again modern feeling has declared itself with no uncertain sound. The *House of Fame* gives us the metre of Gay or Swift; the *Pearl* reappears in *Christabel*, and is thus the ancestor of the *Sensitive Plant* and of some of the rhythms of Swinburne himself. Regularity is a good thing, but a dull uniformity is another; and—though the *House of Fame* is in reality not so uniform as it looks to a casual observer—it is yet the forerunner of those mechanically regular poems with which later generations were wearied.

That the romantic ballads, on which the Host in the *Canterbury Tales* expresses himself so forcibly, had in them a germ of good metre and even of good poetry, is shown by the fact that as early as the days of Sir Thomas Wyatt, and as late as those of our grandfathers, Chaucer's parody of them was taken as a serious poem and duly admired: nay, it is possible that even now there are some who, if they would confess the truth, would

> praise Sir Thopas for a noble tale

whether or not they would

scorn the story that the Knight told.

The merits of this old ballad-style, denied by Chaucer, thus shine even through his travesty; and we for our part are not ashamed to own to a certain liking for *Sir Eglamour*, *Sir Isumbras*, and others of the same class. It may well be that there were too many of them in Chaucer's time, and that the sameness of style and language in them might fret and annoy an artistic taste; but impartial critics may be excused if they do not like to think what we should have missed if the old ballads had been lost altogether.

Again, if the specially English lyric form, such as is exemplified by *Alisoun* or by *Spring is come to town*, had utterly vanished—as apparently it would have done if Chaucer had had his way—we should have lost much that could not easily have been restored; and assuredly Chaucer himself provided no satisfactory substitute. Amid the multitude of "Complaints" and "Balades" which are to be found among his works, there is not one that is not heavy and slow-moving in comparison with these exquisite little songs; and the love-passages in *Troilus*, beautiful as some of them are, lose in daintiness what they gain in dignity by being written in a more solid metre. Nor is there reason to imagine that among the lost "ympnes, roundels, and virelayes," which Chaucer tells us he wrote, were any that in lightness and delicacy were worthy to be compared with *Alisoun.*

Of Chaucer's other technical excellences, of his exactness in rhyme, of his conduct of a story, of his sense of balance and proportion, we could, if this were the time, say much. Much also might be said of his humour, his genial satire, his sly innuendo and polished irony—but these are not *poetical* traits. There is something of far more importance than any of these, of which we find traces in some of the later predecessors of Chaucer, and far more than traces in many of the poets we call for convenience "Anglo-Saxon." In them there was a depth of *imagination*, and a sympathetic, interpretative love of nature, to which we can discover no parallel in Chaucer, and for the like of which we have to wait till the appearance of Wordsworth and Shelley. As we have hinted, much of this imaginative power was absent in the alliterative poets of Chaucer's time; but no small measure is to be found in the author of *Gawain and the Green Knight*, and a little in *Piers the Plowman*. The greater Anglo-Saxon poets, in fact, resembled the Elizabethans in power, in wealth of language, in the free use of metaphor—and also in their lawlessness and profusion. Their followers, with a few noble exceptions, exhibited more of their faults than of their merits; and by the middle of the fourteenth century the merits had almost wholly disappeared. A reaction against the extravagances of the school was desirable and inevitable, precisely as a reaction against the decayed Elizabethans was desirable and inevitable; and Chaucer led the reaction. But, like the Restoration and Augustan poets, he carried the reaction too far. In his devotion to form and comeliness, he failed to see how much genius often lay behind the uncouth outside of the poets whose wildness he wished to prune; and he cleared away the good along with the bad. He deserves, far more than Pope, the praise of "correctness"; and he has a hundred gifts besides which Pope had not; but in a very important sense he did the work that Pope did after him. Fearful of falling, he would not soar; and he remains therefore not one of the first or imaginative class of poets, but the chief of the second—the class to which Pope, Dryden, Horace, Boileau belong. Despite occasional flashes in *Troilus*, it is hardly possible to find a single sustained blaze of the higher imagination in the whole of Chaucer. In Cynewulf, on the other hand, such flashes abound; and at times we find them not only marvellously illuminating, but also continuous. How much of this imagination is Cynewulf's own, and how much is due to the heathenism of which he and his compeers were heirs, is not here an important question. Our point is not that Cynewulf, or any one of these older poets, was in himself a greater genius than Chaucer, but that the older *school* had qualities which Chaucer lacked, and which were not reproduced till at least a century after his time. And, be it observed, these qualities are *English*; they spring from the deepest roots of the English character, and emerge constantly when the English mind is deeply stirred. They appear in English poetry before Chaucer, and they reappear long after Chaucer's death; they have nothing to do with form, with artistic construction, with metrical skill; they cannot be learnt from the example of any poet, but must be born in the man that has them. In Chaucer they were not born.

This may seem a hard saying; it is at any rate a bold one. For Chaucer has attracted the admiration not merely of philologers and students, not merely of critics, but of poets; and of poets not merely of Dryden's class, but of Spenser's and Morris's. It is difficult to believe that such judges can have been mistaken. And yet mistaken we believe they were; they mistook charm for imaginativeness; and the charm of Chaucer is undeniable. But it is not a highly poetical charm; it is that of Herodotus combined with that of Horace, and when we analyse our emotions we find he has delighted us without illuminating us.

We might take, as illustrations of our point, the treatment of the sea in the poetry of Chaucer as compared with its treatment in the Anglo-Saxon poets. And here Stopford Brooke, in his chapter on this latter subject (*Early English Literature*, chap. x), has saved us much trouble. Let anyone, after reading that chapter, take up the *Man of Law's Tale*, and then deny if he can the immense loss that the poetry of the sea has sustained in passing from Caedmon and Cynewulf to Chaucer. Where in Chaucer is there anything like the description of Beowulf's swimming match with Breca, or that of the Red Sea in *Exodus*, or that of the voyage in the *Andreas*? It may be said, of course, that thus to describe the sea did not come in Chaucer's way. But we answer that if he had been a Cynewulf it *would* have come in his way. For in the *Elene* and in the *Guthlac* there was far less chance than in the story of Constance for a description of the sea; and yet what did not Cynewulf make of his chances when they came! Here is a brief passage from *Guthlac*:

Urged the Stallion of the wave, and the Water-rusher ran,
Snell beneath the sorrow-laden. Shone the blazing sky,
Blickering o'er the Burg-halls. Fled the Billow-wood along
Gay and gleaming on the path! Laden, to the hithe,
Flew at speed the Flood-horse, till the Floater of the tide,
After the sea-playing, surged upon the sea-land,
Ground against the shingle-grit.

The mere "kennings" and personifications—the "House of Geofon" for the sea, the "yþa geþraec" for the crashing of the waves, the "waeter-egesa" or Terror of the Waters, which rises before the sailors on their voyage, the Fortress of the Deep (*lager-faesten*) impregnable to the boldest—all these, so common and so striking in the Old English poets, have vanished, when we come to Chaucer, as if they had never been; and he must be strangely destitute of poetic feeling who does not regret their loss. The long-drawn simile, which Chaucer and his school used somewhat freely, is indeed a poor substitute for the packed and concentrated fullness of the old metaphorical "kenning"; and for the old amazing richness and variety of vocabulary no substitute has ever been sought. "Never again," says God to Noah in *Genesis*, "will I lead the Host of Aegir over the dry land"—but to the Chaucerians Aegir and his host are alike dead, and it is but the *wilde wawes* and the *wynd* and *weder*, poor impersonal creatures from which all life has long since departed, that drive Constance forward on her dull voyage. Doubtless she looked up to the stars and saw the moon; but the stars were not to her, as to Cynewulf, the candles of heaven; still less was the moon "wight wonderfully carrying booty between his horns, cunningly adorned, yea, carrying booty home from his raids and his harryings; but driven into dark hiding-places by a wight yet more wondrous, who stealeth from him his prey." Like St Andrew, she is preserved in the waters by a divine sailor, but the sailor, apparently, does not care to talk about his cruises, nor is there one word from first to last to show that the poet who tells the tale has any feeling for either the beauty or the horror of the sea. How different

is all this from the life and vigour of the descriptions
and the conversations in the *Andreas*!

> Then was sorely troubled,
> Sorely wrought the whale-mere. Wallowed there the Horn-
> fish,
> Glode the great deep through, and the gray-backed gull
> Slaughter-greedy wheeled. Dark the storm-sun grew,
> Waxed the winds up, grinded waves;
> Stirred the surges, groaned the cordage,
> Wet with breaking sea. Water-horror rose
> With the might of troops. Then the thegns
> Cold with terror grew, nor thought any one
> That alive he should win at last the land!

Still more clearly felt would be the loss should the
reader turn to the so-called Fourth Riddle on the
Hurricane—whether this be by Cynewulf or by
another—or to the noble elegy called the *Seafarer*.
It is safe to say that nothing like these poems was
written in English between the Conquest and the
French Revolution. No one, surely, can read the
description of the "mighty warrior, compelled to
rest by his commander, driven into darkness, pressed
down in prison, then let loose from thraldom,
thrusting his way outward, till he stirs up the stream-
ings of the sea, and the sea-men shout aloud in fear,
expecting lest the sea should bear their ship to its
grim hour of death"—no one, surely, can read this
poem without feeling that its writer had *seen* the
storm, and had entered into its very soul. In the
union of intense realism and high imagination, in-

deed, even the storm-scenes in the *Tempest* and in
Pericles hardly equal the *Hurricane* and the *Seafarer*; and Stopford Brooke is right in seeking
the nearest parallel to them in Shelley's immortal
Ode to the West Wind. If, then, the absence, during
a long period of years, of an imaginative treatment
of the sea in English poetry be due to Chaucer,
Chaucer has indeed a heavy load to bear.

It may be objected that Chaucer was not, like
Cynewulf and these other poets, acquainted with the
sea. He was, it may be said, essentially a landsman:
even his journeys to Italy had been by land, and
Ocean's varying moods were unknown to him:
apart from a few crossings from Dover to Calais
and back on calm days, he knew nothing of the sea.
It may be so; but almost any other great natural
element will serve our purpose equally well. It will
hardly be denied that Chaucer knew day and night,
or that he was interested in astronomical phenomena.
When the early English poets have to describe night,
they say "Niht helmade," night put on her helm;
when night vanishes, "Nihthelm toglad," the helmet
of night fell apart. When the Wanderer speaks of
winter's terror, he tells how the phantom of night
descends, and hurls from the north her cruel arrows
of hail, to the dread of men. When Guthlac is dying,
night falls violently upon the ornaments of earth.
This is a kind of image which is natural in a time
when heathenism has still left traces of its power. It

is a kind of image which Chaucer not only avoids, but ridicules—

> For the orizonte hath reft the sonne his light—
> This is as muche to seye as it was night;

for his genius was no less the servant of common sense than that of Pope himself, and he carried his reaction against imaginativeness as far as the Augustan poets carried theirs against the violence of the later Elizabethans. The "figure" of personification, indeed, which is the mark of the childhood of the world, and which therefore appears so constantly in the "eternal child" Shelley, scarcely appears in Chaucer at all. We do indeed hear of April "with his showrës sootë percing the drought of Marche"; but what is that to the myriad personifications of Anglo-Saxon poetry? The smitten byrnies sing greedy death-songs; hunger is a pale table-ghost; death is a thief, stepping with stealthy strides, strong and fierce to break into the house of the soul; fire is a raging warrior, rushing on fowls and beasts over all the earth; the swan is carried by the strength of clouds, a spirit faring over flood and field. Personification is the very life and soul of most of those remarkable poems called the *Riddles,* many of which are not merely true and exact descriptions of nature, but also penetrating and sympathetic *assumptions* of her varying moods. It is dangerous to assert a negative; but it is probably true to say that there is not a single reference to nature, of this peculiar kind, in all Chaucer; not one of the kind which Wordsworth would have wished to claim as his own. And all this though no poet that ever lived has loved *external* nature more keenly than Chaucer. He loved to hear "the blisful briddës sing"; the lark, saluting in her song the morning gray, gave him exquisite delight; he was passionately fond of flowers, and he seems to have been extraordinarily sensitive to the "seasons' difference." Spring worked in him as it works upon the young man's fancy. But for him the mysterious scarcely existed; the glamour of twilight touched him with no agitation of the soul; alike in religion and in poetry he was of a practical turn, and had scant sympathy with the world of shadows. What kinship had he then with those old Englishmen who, in their very code of laws, could speak of fire as a "thief," and to whom fever was an elf who rode a man with whip and spur? How could he understand those who spoke of trees and brushwood as the locks upon the head of earth, and to whom the raven, flying over the battle, was a swart Valkyrie, a dark chooser of the slain?

In some of the most beautiful lines in English Chaucer has described his love of books and of the studies from which he could not be drawn until May had come and the flowers began to spring. Elsewhere he tells us that every evening, as soon as his ledger-work was done, he hastened home, and, as dumb as any stone, "sat at another book till fully

daswed was his look." He lived thus "as an her-
myte"; and he had the hermit's reward. But he had
also the hermit's limitations; and they are plainly
visible in his poetry. The bookish man is often a
keen judge of character; and such was Chaucer. But
there is an unmistakable tone about men describing
events "quorum pars magna fuerunt" which marks
them off from men to whom the events are mainly
"copy": and Chaucer was of the latter class. He
could, as we shall see, describe a tournament with
some vigour; but war was not his *métier*. He does,
in the *Legend of Dido*, describe a hunt, and mimics
with a certain amount of spirit the "Go bet!" of the
keepers. But what is that to the fierce enthusiasm
with which the author of *Gawain* pursues the boar
or the stag, and the still fiercer, almost barbaric, joy
with which he assists at the "breaking" of the one
and the "unlacing" of the other? Similarly, no one
would desire a better description than the one which
Chaucer has given—by vivid human touches here
and there—of the road from Southwark to Canterbury; but we look in vain in him for a wild landscape
like that which the peerless knight passed through
on his way from Arthur's court through Wirral to
the Green Chapel, by "misy and mire," where

> The hasil and the hawthorn were harled al samen,
> With roȝe raged mosse rayled aywhere,
> With mony bryddes unblythe upon bare twyges,
> That pitously piped for pine of the colde.

There is nothing in Chaucer like the description of the weltering wastes over which the Wanderer wearily passed; nor, it is needless to say, is there anything in him like that passage in *Beowulf* in which Hrothgar tells of the "unhéoru stów" where Grendel dwelt, that eerie place from which even the hunted stag turned back, and which he would face death rather than approach. Chaucer, like L'Allegro, was most at home in towered cities and amid the busy hum of men; he did not tread easily in haunted spots.

It may be answered that *of course* his range is not universal; that no one poet can deal with every possible theme; and that the question is not how many subjects the poet treats, but the degree of insight and genius with which he treats those he has made his own. Precisely; but the question at issue is the genius of earlier poets than Chaucer, and the extent of his influence upon later poets. If, then, we find earlier poets showing unquestioned genius in *their* themes, which are different from Chaucer's; and if we find later poets working, with more or less success, in regions which Chaucer never visited, we are entitled to say English poetry has been less influenced by him than is usually asserted. But further, in these mysterious and mighty themes lies precisely the favourite field of the truly great poet. There is something in the very choice of subject which marks out the *supreme* poet from his fellows. It is not an accident that Coleridge chose to write of *diablerie* and witchcraft; the great theme beckoned to the great poet. It is not a mere chance that Swinburne could not keep his thoughts from the sea; the stronger the movement of his poetic inspiration the more it sought an adequate sphere in which to play. Thus the fact that Chaucer's subjects are in the main of the earth, earthy, is significant of the limits of his poetic genius.

But even within the range of the subjects of his choice, his treatment is not that of the supreme poet; he does not lift common things into the ethereal realm. Sometimes this is due to a want of full sympathy. He had, for instance, seen war; but it is plain that at heart he was no more a warrior than Horace. His battle-pieces lack reality, and are at best descriptions of the *statue* of Mars. The combats of Palamon and Arcite, and the tourneys in which Lycurgus and Emetrius distinguish themselves, are adorned with the requisite number of similes and digressions, but are even less the real thing than Virgil's war-pictures. We soon feel them to be mere contests of chivalry, with none of the fury of a pitched and deadly battle. Contrast them with the conflict in which the Huns were put to flight by Constantine (*Elene*, 109 sq.):

Loud before the troops the trumpets sang;
The raven rejoiced in the work,
Dewy-feathered the eagle looked down on the march,
On the war of the cruel ones; the wolf raised a song,
That dweller in the holt: the battle-Terror stood;

There was the crash of the shields and the meeting of heroes,
Hard swinging of hands, and the fall of men,
Since first they met the flight of arrows.
On that fey folk flew showers of darts,
Spears over the yellow shield-hedge; among the crowd of foes
Shot the grim haters; battle-snakes hurled they
With the force of their fingers forth on the foe.

In those words is the true ring: the writer was either an actual fighter or one who, like Scott, would have been a fighter if he could. But still more true are the battle-pieces in *Judith*, in the poem on Maldon, and even in the inferior *Battle of Brunanburh*, which Tennyson's translation has made familiar to all. Whatever these poems may lack, they have at least reality.

Of love-poems in the Old English, time has left us but few. This is not to say that few they always were. We know *Beowulf* but through one manuscript, and most of the poems in the Exeter Book through another; *Elene* and *Andreas* through a third: there must have been many that were never committed to writing, and many more whose manuscripts have perished. To judge by the analogy of Icelandic poetry, love-poems in Anglo-Saxon were neither few nor feeble. One of those remaining to us, *The Wife's Complaint*, we can discern through its many obscurities to have been a poem of extraordinary intensity and directness. It was obviously—its very obscurity proves this—inspired by an actual situation, and was almost certainly written by the heroine herself or by someone marvellously capable of entering into her feelings. It is, in a word, a *genuine* poem through and through—as genuine as one of Burns's to Mary or one of Goethe's to Lili—and Chaucer's laboured *Complaints to Pity* and the like have as much right to be compared with it as Pope's *Eloisa to Abelard* has to be compared with Shakespeare's Sonnets. "*Fair Ruthless*" and Rosamund have precisely as much reality as Horace's Lalages and Pyrrhas. In *Troilus*, it is true, Chaucer has written a genuine love-poem: but of another class. The comparison here is not with any extant English poem, but rather with one—if such there ever was—in which an Old English poet had told a tale similar to that of *Laxdaela* or *Gunnlaug's Saga*. In *Troilus* Chaucer all but lifts himself into the region of the romantic poets of modern days; it is the one work of his in which he seems to have surveyed the Promised Land from afar; and after it he turned back for ever. Or, to use the image applied by Macaulay to Dryden, in *Troilus* Chaucer made his nearest approach to Oromasdes; but Arimanes carried him off.

That in occasional flights of *sublimity* Old English poetry was very rich, is a proposition that needs no proving to those who know *Judith*, or *Christ*, or the *Ruin*, or certain parts of *Genesis*. Sublimity, indeed, is a markedly English characteristic; and our literature is probably rivalled in this respect by the Hebrew alone. Sublimity invariably seems to start forth when there is, under any shape or form, a revival of poetry in England. Even Wordsworth, for example, though determined to "make poetry speak the language of common life," puts forth the sublime *Tintern Abbey* in the very volume meant to teach the lesson of humility. Francis Thompson, again, when poetry was becoming too much the slave of mere technique, burst out with the sublime *Hound of Heaven*. When allied with a sense of form, as it was allied in Milton, English sublimity produces some of the most stupendous effects to be found in the whole range of literature. Unfortunately, when not so allied, it easily degenerates into bombast; and so it too often did degenerate in early English poetry. There is much that is turgid, in the midst of much that is noble, in *Beowulf* and in the *Christ*. As we come further down the stream of time, the turgidity passes over into noisy feebleness, often weakening into mere absurdity. Even in *Gawain*, the author of which possessed a genius for the sublime not equalled till we reach Spenser, sublimity runs very close to futility. In that poem, the very theme lies perilously near the ridiculous, and the treatment, if often very lofty, is often low and creeping; precisely as, in the same author's *Pearl*, some of the most exquisite passages ever written alternate with dull theological disquisitions[1].

[1] I agree with Palgrave (*Landscape in Poetry*, p. 116) that in *Pearl* it is not simple Nature on which the poet's eye was fixed: he paints a

It was this turgidity, doubtless, that struck Chaucer, whose sense of the ridiculous was marvellously acute; and it was this that, at least in all his mature work, he avoided with the utmost care. There are sublime passages in *Troilus*, such for instance as "O blisful light" at the beginning of the third canto; but every one of them, without exception, is borrowed from Boccaccio, Petrarch, or another. There is a very sublime passage in the *Second Nun's Tale*; but that is from Dante. Many other more or less elevated passages are versifications of Boethius, whose great work Chaucer knew nearly by heart. The *Knight's Tale* might easily have aimed at the sublime; it never really rises higher than the stately and the dignified.

Elsewhere we find Chaucer approaching the sublime only in order to run away from it with a laugh —much after the ironical fashion in which Horace shuns epic majesty in his *Odes*. For Chaucer, whose motto was emphatically μηδὲν ἄγαν, was more afraid of falling than desirous of scaling the heights. Like many men with a lively sense of humour, he saw so keenly how near the sublime is to the ridiculous, that to avoid the latter he shunned the former. This

supernatural landscape similar to the Italian Gardens of Love. Nevertheless the peculiar *imaginativeness* of the poem is something beyond the reach of Chaucer. Palgrave truly remarks that "there is probably no great poet to whom man was the proper subject for man more exclusively than Chaucer. Hence his voluminous work but sparingly represents Nature and Landscape."

was the secret of the mock-modesty with which he ascribes anything particularly daring to some "Lollius" or other "author" on whom he prefers to shift the responsibility for a specially lofty flight. And there can be no doubt that, at the time at which he appeared, the moderating influence he exerted was almost wholly for good. His own avoidance of puns, conceits, and "high-falutin," was a precious example in days when such things were taken as the greatest of merits: and the Elizabethans show how easily such sins beset the most powerful of minds when not regulated by impeccable good taste. But still the fact remains that sublimity—so marked a feature in English poetry at its best—is hardly to be found in Chaucer and owes little to him. It is no blame to him that he did not aim at what he could not reach, and did not try to give that which he did not possess; but it would be a serious disparagement to English poetry if we were to believe that its capacities were limited to those paths in which he led the way.

It may well be asked, as we thus proceed, what after all, in our opinion, *was* the contribution which Chaucer made to English poetry. For it is obviously not our intention to disparage him; and yet so far we have done little in the way of praise. We have allowed his gift for characterisation, but such a gift is not that of a poet as such; it is often possessed in the highest measure by men of no poetical talent at

all, like Fielding, for instance, or Balzac. His gift
for narrative, again, proves nothing as to his natural
poetic equipment. He did, it is true, enrich the
language with many new and fruitful metres; but
metrical skill, though a pleasant addition to other
poetic endowments, is far from the highest of such
gifts. What then has he done for us? Much every
way; chiefly in this, that he taught English poets,
both by precept and by example, the necessity of
form: of balance, of order, and of construction. As
an artist, he is all but incomparable; the more closely
he is studied, the more does his artistic merit come
to view. And his influence, in this regard, upon
subsequent writers has been of incalculable value.
Compare those men who came before him with
those who succeeded—and note the difference. The
Scottish school owes almost everything to Chaucer.
Observe the *widening* effect of Chaucerianism upon
a true but small poet like Henryson, and its *restrain-
ing* effect upon a great but somewhat wild and irregular genius like Dunbar. It is true that it did little to
curb the long-windedness of Lydgate, or to har-
monise the jog-trot stanzas of Hoccleve; but imagine
Lydgate writing in the style of *Piers the Plowman*,
or Hoccleve's *De Regimine Principum* in the metre
of *Richard the Redeless*! Above all, consider the
debt of Spenser to Chaucer, so nobly acknowledged!
To say nothing of the Hymns and other poems in
which Rhyme Royal is used, or of the obligation to

Chaucer for the Spenserian stanza itself, with all its varied beauties and immense range, the *art* in the *Faerie Queene*, if largely due to the Italian masters and to the Latin and Greek classics, is mainly derived from *Troilus* and the *Canterbury Tales*. Spenser's cast of mind was different from Chaucer's, but precisely where his restraint and self-discipline are greatest, there his poem is at its best, and there we can most easily trace the Chaucerian spirit surviving in his disciple. Thus Elizabethan poetry, where most artistic, harks back to Chaucer; and thus succeeding literature, with all its derivations from the Elizabethan, leads us back to Chaucer also. This is great praise, and it is deserved. Those alone truly depreciate Chaucer who try to claim for him still more.

ii

IN Shakespearean study, as in the study of any classical writer whose "canon" is not yet definitively decided, the lower or textual criticism ought to precede the higher or aesthetic. Whether these two functions be united in one person, or, as is usually the case, distributed to two, this is the only logical order. Perhaps the main problem of the student of any great author is to discover the man; and by this we do not mean to discover the man as husband, as father, as citizen, or as politician, but the man as artist, the man as creator of the works. And for this purpose the first necessity is to find out what the man actually wrote, to unearth as far as possible his *ipsissima verba*, and to sever from his authentic writings any spurious accretions. To form some conception of the Proto-Isaiah one must set aside the prophecies of the Deutero-Isaiah. Simple and even platitudinous as this may seem, it would have been as well if all critics of our Elizabethan literature had regularly borne it in mind. For example, it would have been desirable for Swinburne, before plunging into a rhapsody about the phrase "helly spout" of blood, to discover what the textual critic (Swinburne himself, it may be, or another) had to say of it. The phrase may or may not be the height of sublimity; but in either case, if what the author really wrote was not "helly spout" but "Hellespont," the rhapsody will have to be re-written. Similarly, the lines in *A Lover's Complaint*[1],

> O father, what a hell of witchcraft lies
> In the small orb of one particular tear,

may or may not deserve the praise that has been lavished upon them; but, till the textual critic has decided upon their authorship, it is vain to take them into consideration in appraising Shakespeare's poetry.

Towards the accomplishment of this most important task, much progress has been made. In certain cases, indeed, the work is remarkably easy. When Shakespeare is truly himself, no trained ear can fail to recognise his authentic voice. No one has ever wished to ascribe to some Middleton or Rowley the words of the Duke to Claudio, or the words of Lear to Cordelia as he wakes from his sleep. On the other hand, there are passages in Shakespeare's so-called works so un-Shakespearean in tone and style, that the dullest of critics, as soon as the possibility of alien authorship is suspected, at once assigns them to another hand. Such are nearly the whole of *Henry VI*, and at least the first two Acts of *Pericles*. Between these two classes of passages no confusion is possible: the one bears the birth-

[1] In my opinion, probably Chapman's.

mark of Shakespeare, the other every sign of the supposititious. The spuriousness of the latter, indeed, would have been asserted two centuries ago, had the literary history of Shakespeare's time been known. Dryden, for example, accepted *Pericles* only on the assumption that it was Shakespeare's earliest work. Yet even now, it is to be feared, not all aesthetic critics, when they try to form an image of the artist Shakespeare, take pains to separate the spurious from the genuine.

In other cases, the task of textual criticism has been harder. It is sometimes far from easy to distinguish the good work of inferior men from the less inspired work of greater men. Thus, for instance, a certain poem was for centuries ascribed to Virgil which Professor Skutsch has shown good reason for giving to Gallus. Hundreds of other examples might be adduced. Nevertheless, difficult as discrimination in such cases is, the task, as regards Shakespeare, has during the last fifty or eighty years been accomplished with more or less success. For example, the Fletcherian parts of *Henry VIII*, some of them not unworthy of Shakespeare, have been marked off and assigned to their rightful owner: and it is possible that the "last word" may soon be said on the similar problems of the *Two Noble Kinsmen, Sir Thomas More*, or *Edward III*. And a pity it is that this work was not done sooner! Some grotesque errors would have been saved to the aesthetic critics.

"The character of Wolsey," wrote Hazlitt in 1817, "the description of his pride and of his fall, are inimitable, and have, besides their gorgeousness of effect, a pathos which *only the genius of Shakespear* could lend to the distresses of a proud, bad man, like Wolsey....Nor is the account which Griffith gives of Wolsey's death *less Shakespearian*."

About this it is sufficient to say that of the passages which describe Wolsey's pride and his fall, and of Griffith's account of his death, Shakespeare in all probability wrote not a line.

But there remains a whole series of questions compared with which those just referred to, difficult and complicated as they have often proved, are simple. To the man who wishes to disinter the real Shakespeare it is not enough, in dealing with the mass of literature which has come down under that name, thus to separate the wholly genuine from the wholly spurious. There remains a large territory which is strictly neither spurious nor genuine, but in a sense both at once: and it is this very region that has been the least satisfactorily explored, and that contains the most dangerous pitfalls for the student of Shakespeare's "mind and art." No competent writer will to-day make a mistake like that just quoted from Hazlitt; nor will he see, with Charles Knight, a profound and subtle psychological meaning in the ascription to Feste of the nonsense-verses at the end of *Twelfth Night* [1] : but he is still liable to mistakes

---

[1] Yet Stopford Brooke, in his *Ten More Plays of Shakespeare*, p. 57, shows a leaning to this heresy. "Wherever it (*Twelfth Night*) is played

intrinsically no less absurd, though their absurdity may be for ever hidden by our ignorance. Dogmatism, in any case, must be shunned like the plague.

First, then, the question of Elizabethan "authorship," in all its forms, has never been thoroughly investigated, and will perhaps always resist solution. But there are many indications that authorship in Shakespeare's time—indeed at all times till quite recently—was very far from the single and definite thing that it is in ours. How much, for example, that goes under the name of Euripides really belongs to Cephisophon? How much of *Piers the Plowman* is really the work of another than Langland? Not only had the sin of plagiarism not yet been invented; the selection of an author's name for a title-page was often merely a matter of chance or convenience, and a work ascribed to a particular person might actually have as many writers as "Henry VIII's" answer to Luther, or "Boyle's" refutation of Bentley. Shakespeare, for instance, was the most popular author of his age, and it was a profitable device of piratical booksellers to issue all sorts of farragoes under his name, or, with a touch of caution, under his initials. Thus the *Passionate Pilgrim*, in which there is but the smallest proportion of Shakespeare's genuine

or read, it is part of the great world of man. And perhaps the last verse of the song, with which the Clown closes it, means to tell that truth." The song is probably the merest gag, to which the clown had licence to add what he pleased: and if the words have a profound meaning here, they have it also in *Lear* (III. ii).

work, was issued as his by Jaggard in 1599. In this case, it is true, the author was for once roused to remonstrance, with the result that in a later impression the offending title was removed; but this has not prevented writers—some, like Dean Church, of high repute—from quoting as Shakespeare's certain verses by Barnfield or Bartholomew Griffin. Sometimes, especially after Shakespeare's death, publishers seem to have acted with still less justification than Jaggard: and even in his lifetime the six spurious plays of the Third Folio were unscrupulously ascribed to him. It would be hard indeed to detect in the *Yorkshire Tragedy* a dozen lines that Shakespeare can have written; and in *Thomas Lord Cromwell* perhaps fewer still would now be regarded as bearing any sign of genius: yet the publisher's certificates imposed on the Schlegels and Tiecks two hundred years later. Nor was it always the piratical bookseller who acted thus. In the Folio of 1623, the authorised edition of Shakespeare's works, we find the three parts of *Henry VI* ascribed to him when, in all likelihood, his only connection with them was to assist Marlowe in the revision. It would be a weary work merely to enumerate those who have been misled into thinking Shakespeare responsible for the horrible travesty of Joan of Arc in this play. Similarly, the First Folio includes *Titus Andronicus*, in which—despite the vigorous advocacy of Churton Collins and others—the majority of critics will

decline to credit Shakespeare with more than a score
or two of lines at the utmost.

With examples like these before us, we refuse to
regard the inclusion of a play in the First Folio as
any proof whatever that it is, or was viewed by
Heminge and Condell as being, exclusively Shakespeare's. To them, Shakespeare was its author in the
Elizabethan sense; that is, he had a hand in it. He
had written it as Jonson had written *Eastward Ho*,
or as Buckingham afterwards wrote the *Rehearsal*.
How often, being pressed for time, or for some other
reason, Shakespeare chartered another playwright to
help him out with the more mechanical parts of his
work, will probably never be known; but it ought
constantly to be before the minds of his critics as a
possibility. That Dumas did this regularly is of course
well known; that Shakespeare, who in a certain royal
carelessness as to his rights and in indifference to
fame, resembled Dumas, did it also, is a matter, not
indeed of proof, but of plausible inference. Scarcely
any other hypothesis will explain the phenomena
of *Timon of Athens*; we have already mentioned
Pericles; and many good critics would thus account
for some phenomena in *Troilus and Cressida*. But,
in the case of *Timon* at least, the collaborators were
such poor artists that the inferiority of their work is
obvious, and the sutures palpable. In the case of
Pericles the inferiority is equally manifest; and there
is little doubt where the work of Shakespeare stops

and that of his helpers begins. But what if on occasion he obtained the aid of a writer of greater merit —as he obtained that of Fletcher in *Henry VIII*— or of a man not necessarily original in genius, but capable of successfully mimicking the style of his betters? Such writers have abounded in every age. In that case, the sutures would *not* be palpable; the point of junction would often be as difficult of detection as in the novels of Erckmann-Chatrian, or as in Wilkie Collins's *Blind Love*, which was completed by Walter Besant from a point on which no critic ever succeeded in alighting. That *we* could not perceive the work of a collaborator would not prove he did not exist, but merely that he was very good at his trade. Of some passages we could say with certainty, "These *are* Shakespeare's"; of a very few, "These are *not* his"; of a good many, "These may be his or they may not"; of yet others, "These are somebody else's, revised by him."

Thus, for example, in a play which has given rise to suspicion in many minds—the tragedy of *Macbeth*—there are scores of passages which it is certain, if there is any aesthetic certainty in the world, that no one but Shakespeare could have written. There are also some, like the speech of the English doctor about the King's Evil, or like the speech of Hecat, which it assuredly did not require a Shakespearean genius to compose. But there is one passage—the long dialogue between Malcolm and Macduff in

Act IV—which occupies a middle position. It is most certainly not very good; and yet in style it is not altogether un-Shakespearean. It is, in fact, precisely such a passage as a good workman could have written under Shakespeare's direction. The materials lay ready in Holinshed, requiring but certain omissions here and a little emphasis there to make them suitable for their purpose of explaining a certain development in the action of the play. What more likely than that Shakespeare lent his copy of Holinshed to some playwright, and bade him hitch the prose into blank verse, afterwards, perhaps, touching up the work here and there? For, in his later years especially, Shakespeare was in no want of money, and could easily have spared far more than the usual pittance which writers like Day, Drayton, or Munday were fain to accept from a manager like Henslowe. But if this be the case, adequate criticism of this part of the play must obviously be a very delicate matter. Similar remarks, *mutatis mutandis*, apply to the earlier scene of the wounded soldier—a scene which has often staggered its readers[1].

In some such way, also, we may very possibly account for the presence in the *Tempest* of the rhymed Masque, which, whatever its merits or de-

---

[1] Neither of these scenes suggests Middleton as the author: there are plain marks of Shakespeare *here and there*, and plain marks of a bad writer almost everywhere.

I am strongly inclined to believe that Mr J. M. Robertson has proved at least that one of the collaborators in *Timon of Athens* was Chapman.

merits, is just the kind of thing which a journeyman can do as well as a genius. The Masque in *Cymbeline*, again, is so poor that in mercy to Shakespeare many critics have refused to regard a line of it as his; and much the same may be said of the Chorus in *Winter's Tale*. Everything, in fact, seems to indicate that now and then, whether from weariness, from charity, or from lack of time, Shakespeare passed on certain pieces of work to others.

All this of course, in the absence of external evidence, must be treated as matter of conjecture merely; but Shakespeare had another collaborator whose existence is not shadowy or conjectural, but substantial and absolutely certain. This collaborator was no one else than the author of the raw material on which Shakespeare based his play. That author appears in many forms. Now, as in the case of *Hamlet*, he is a tolerably accomplished playwright like Kyd: now, as in the case of *Measure for Measure*, a poor drudge like Whetstone. Sometimes he is an actual man, though utterly unknown, like the author of the *Famous Victories of Henry V*; sometimes he is a mere abstraction, like tradition or history, or even stage convention. But in every case he worked along with Shakespeare, sometimes hindering him, sometimes inspiring him; and it is impossible to separate the real Shakespeare without taking into full account this too much neglected coadjutor. A few examples may make our point clear.

Shakespeare has often been praised for the way in which he makes Angelo succumb to the temptation of Isabella's purity. He who would have been quite above the assaults of a Bianca, or even of a Cleopatra, yields to the attractions of an "enskied and sainted" votarist. But the same point is made in *Promos and Cassandra*; and all that Shakespeare does is to enlarge and improve upon the hint that Whetstone had given him[1]. Again, what torrents of panegyric have been poured upon the speech of Katharine of Aragon at the trial (in *Henry VIII*)! The speech is indeed admirable, and deserves all the praise it has received; but it is not Shakespeare's. It is taken, with very little change, from Holinshed.

Somewhat similar, though different in certain obvious respects, is the phenomenon presented by the equally admirable speech of Ulysses in *Troilus and Cressida*, on "degree." Here Shakespeare parts company entirely with the work on which the play as a whole is founded: there is nothing, for instance, in Chaucer corresponding to this speech, and nothing, so far as we know, in any of the settings of the legend which the dramatist may have consulted for the purposes of his play. Yet it is not original; and

[1] That Shakespeare, again, deliberately *meant* a contrast between Romeo's "love" for Rosaline and his passion for Juliet, though probable, has to be decided from a general study of his mind and art, and not from the play by itself; for, as Halliwell-Phillipps pointed out, the Rosaline story is in Brooke. This, the reader will remember, is fully recognised by Professor Bradley (*Oxford Lectures on Poetry*, p. 326, note).

here again he pursues his authority a little further than strict dramatic propriety would have demanded.

Alike for this speech, and for the very similar harangue in that part of *Sir Thomas More* which is generally ascribed to Shakespeare, a source has often been sought in Sir John Cheke's *Hurt of Sedition* (1549). To us it seems far more probable that Shakespeare, for both discourses, went elsewhere. We regard them both as almost certainly based on a reminiscence of Sir Thomas Elyot's *Governour*, in which we find the importance of *ordre* exhibited after much more Shakespearean fashion than it is by Cheke. The reader, however, may easily form his own conclusions. "Take away ordre from all thynges," says Elyot, "what shulde than remayne? certes nothynge finally, except some man wolde imagine eftsones *Chaos*: which of some is expounde a confuse *mixture*." "This *Chaos*, when degree is suffocate," says Ulysses, "follows the choking"; and shortly before he has said, "When the planets, *in evil mixture*, to disorder wander, what plagues divert and rend!"

But whether the speech of Ulysses be from Elyot or from Cheke—and it is not impossible that Shakespeare had both in his mind—what we are to notice, if we would rightly study him, is not the dramatic appropriateness of the speech (that of More is far truer *dramatically* than that of Ulysses), but the way in which Shakespeare's mind, seizing upon a passage which struck him, worked it up into poetry, and grew gradually more and more excited by the poetic impulse, until it carried him far beyond the requirements of the play. In blunt language, Shakespeare "let himself go"; and we would not have it otherwise. But the result, though an admirable piece of declamation, is appropriate neither to the mind of the Homeric age, nor to the feudal mind that produced the medieval romance of Troy. It is Shakespeare, first finding that someone else has expressed his own ideas, and then waxing eloquent on his own account.

The death—whether we call it a murder or an execution—of Rosencrantz and Guildenstern has always been a stumbling-block to those critics who view Hamlet as a man of intellect though paralysed by weakness of will. With it we have dealt elsewhere, and have, we hope, shown that it is but the retention of an essential portion of the old legend, when such retention was aesthetically inappropriate but necessary to satisfy the audience. In the enthusiasm of composition Shakespeare had developed Hamlet into a character quite incapable of committing such a deed, and then—he awoke to the remembrance that the deed, being part of a familiar plot, had to be committed nevertheless. It is therefore futile for the critics to worry about it. As well ask what *artistic* reason Scott had for bringing Athelstane to life again, or for the broken plot of *St Ronan's Well*. The reasons were cogent, but altogether unliterary, like many a "happy ending" in a novel. Nor is this by any means the only case where such external motives may be suspected. Indeed, all through *Hamlet*, in especial, the critic has to be on his guard. How much is Shakespeare, and how much is Kyd—if Kyd be really the author of the original Hamlet play? Some scholars think, with Professor Boas, that we have in the First Quarto a more or less garbled version of *Hamlet* as Kyd left it. If so, many things often ascribed to Shakespeare and praised as his are not his at all. But even if Professor Boas is wrong, it is more than likely that much in our *Hamlet* is really part of the older play. There are, for example, many Senecan maxims which may well be due to an admirer and imitator of Seneca, such as Kyd is known to have been. "There is nothing good nor bad but thinking makes it so" is Seneca all over. "Levis est dolor, si nihil illi opinio adiecerit," says Seneca in his seventy-eighth Epistle, "levem illum, dum putas, facies; ad opinionem dolemus." And the Ghost, that very Senecan creation, is almost certainly Kyd's[1].

It may of course be said that Shakespeare, in revising Kyd's play, treated it with freedom, altering, adding, rejecting, and in fact making the whole

---

[1] An equally close parallel has, it is true, been found in the famous saying of Boethius, repeatedly imitated by Chaucer, "Adeo nihil est miserum nisi cum putes" (*Consol. Phil.* Book II, prose 4): cp. Chaucer's *Fortune,*   "No man is wrecched, but himself it wene."
But Boethius doubtless drew it, in his turn, from Seneca: in any case our argument is but slightly affected.

material his own. To this we reply that nothing is more capricious than revision. When Shakespeare once began altering, he would unquestionably continue; one alteration would lead to another, and he would gradually be carried through a whole scene. But before he warmed to the task, or later, when his hand or his mind had chilled again, he would leave alone many a line which otherwise he would have mended: and even an inconsistency, if not very gross, would not fret him sufficiently to set him writing. Much, in fact, of the older play would remain almost entirely untouched. It has already occurred to many writers that possibly the famous "tables" speech of Hamlet—

> My tables—meet it is I set it down—

was thus carelessly retained, without change or revision, from the old play. This we do not believe. Whether originally Kyd's or not, there is in the passage an appropriateness to the situation, and a suitability to Hamlet's character, which we are sure Shakespeare could not miss; and the whole scene bears plain marks of his revising hand. But the conflicting signs of Hamlet's age, which have puzzled commentators for centuries, seem to us impossible of explanation on any hypothesis except the one we are considering—namely, that Shakespeare had another man's work before him, and altered it in some places but not in others. With regard to the allied question as to where Hamlet was at the time of his father's murder, again no other solution seems to us conceivable. In one part of the play every indication seems to show that Hamlet, along with Rosencrantz and Guildenstern, was then at Wittenberg. In other places equally strong indications point to the conclusion that he had left Wittenberg for years, and had long been living at Elsinore, when his father died. And here we are glad to have the powerful support of Professor Bradley (*Shakespearean Tragedy*, p. 406):

> The only solution I can suggest is that, in the story or play which Shakespeare used, Hamlet and the others were all at the time of the murder young students at Wittenberg, and that when he determined to make them older men (or to make Hamlet, at any rate, older) he did not take trouble enough to carry this idea through all the necessary detail, and so left some inconsistencies.

There are many other passages, not only in *Hamlet* but in other plays, in which some such explanation is, in our opinion, imperatively demanded. Shakespeare, like Homer, was occasionally betrayed into "nodding"; and the critic, in his search for the real dramatist, must be very careful to take these weary moments into due account. Shakespeare might almost have been thinking of such lapses of his own when he makes Lear say,

> We are not ourselves
> When nature being oppressed commands the mind
> To suffer with the body;

and the "heady" reader must refuse

> To take the indisposed and sickly fit
> For the sound man.

Readers and hearers of all degrees of taste and intellect, from the rank of a Partridge to that of a Professor Bradley, have boggled at the rejection of Falstaff. But here again we must make the due allowances. That Prince Henry had in his youth been fond of "open haunts and popularity," that he had frequented the tavern and come into awkward collision with the law, was one unalterable tradition. That on ascending the throne he got rid of his loose companions with almost miraculous rapidity, was another. Doubtless, when Shakespeare began *Henry IV*, and plunged into his immortal setting of the former tradition, he had the latter clearly in his mind. But Falstaff, once invented, speedily like a Frankenstein monster dominated his maker, and became, despite all Shakespeare's efforts, the sort of character whom it was an intolerable outrage, both literary and moral, for Henry to reject. Yet that intolerable outrage had to come to pass; for history demanded it; and the "mirror of all Christian kings" flings aside without remorse or scruple his most faithful follower, runs bad humours on him, and kills his heart. This, we are glad to think, is not Shakespeare free, but Shakespeare in chains.

In very similar fashion it behoves us to be on our

guard in dealing with such scenes as that in *Much Ado* in which the Prince and Claudio repudiate Hero. This scene is painful enough in all conscience; but it was probably expected by the audience, for something very like it is to be found in the original novel of Bandello on which the play is based. With regard to Shakespeare's treatment of it one can scarcely better the words of Stopford Brooke:

> I think the ugliness of the conduct of the two men under this central test, and not only the ugliness but their intentional discourtesy, got on Shakespeare's literary nerves, and caused him in this scene not to write so well as usual. When the subject, as in this scene, is wrongly or inadequately conceived, the execution is sure to be inadequately or wrongly done. The artist often does not know that his conception of the thing is wrong till the inadequate execution of his work tells him that something has gone astray. He has been unconscious till this moment of revelation that his original arrangement of the subject was out of truth.

The fact is, that once more the poetic impulse had run away with Shakespeare. The story as he received it easily admitted such an incident; the story as it had been glorified by his genius, and as it had been expanded by the addition of Benedick and Beatrice and all that they imply, had outgrown itself, and had put away childish things. But the incident was still *there*, and had to be included somehow. What wonder that we feel uneasy as we read it?

KR   4

Much the same explanation may be given of the difficulties that confront us as we gaze at the tragic figure of Shylock. To the author of *The Jew*, on which apparently the *Merchant of Venice* was based, Shylock was more or less of a comic character, no more to be pitied when he falls into misfortune than "the roaring Devil in the old play" when his nails are pared with a wooden dagger. Such, doubtless, he was to Shakespeare also when he began his work on the play: and such, there is reason to believe, was he to the original actors even of the *Merchant of Venice* itself. But, as the poet worked on the character, his hand was subdued to what it worked in, and gradually Shylock grew into the wronged and colossal figure in whom, as Heine saw, is summed up "all the martyrdom which, for eighteen centuries, had been borne by a whole tortured people." The comedy is marred; and, though we vastly prefer its present imperfection to the null faultlessness it would have shown if Shakespeare had not "let himself go," yet we must not imagine that, if *absolutely* free, he would have allowed the play to end as it does. He had his audience to consider, which knew the ending and expected it. Had he reprieved Shylock, the groundlings would have felt like a Tyburn mob defrauded of the expected hanging. On the other hand, it was impossible for him to go back in a chilled mood and remove the tragic pathos from Shylock's lamentations. There are some demands of artistry which not the most artistic of poets can bring themselves to satisfy[1].

In *Twelfth Night* there is an instance of a slightly different class. For the great character of Malvolio Shakespeare found no prototype in his "original," Barnabe Rich's novel or the Italian play *Gl' Ingannati*. In all likelihood it was drawn from his own imagination and experience. But it went through much the same transfiguring process as that of Shylock. At first, doubtless, Shakespeare had the idea of making Malvolio a purely comic character; and one, moreover, with whom it would be easy to "bring down the house." As a kind of Puritan, he would be just the man whom the playgoers would delight to see turned into a "notorious geck and gull." But here again the amazing sympathy of the dramatist is speedily enlisted on the side of his creature. The joke palls on its inventor; even Sir Toby cannot pursue it to the upshot, and finally it is left to be carried through by the clown—with whom, as injured by Malvolio, we can feel a counterbalancing sympathy. But no skill can prevent the

---

[1] We may perhaps compare with this the feelings of Virgil as he contemplated the fourth book of the *Aeneid*. Dido had run away with him, and in the process destroyed all respect for the pious Aeneas. Yet Virgil must have known the episode as his masterpiece; and all his artistry, all his care for structure, could not induce him to tamper with the picture, and save the character of his hero. The *Aeneid*, in fact, was ruined by the very beauty of its best part. Doubtless this was the cause of Virgil's despair, and of his wish that the poem should be burnt; for he had entangled himself in a knot which nothing could untie.

sudden jar we experience when, in the midst of all the explanations and reconciliations at the end, Malvolio rushes out with the cry, "I'll be revenged on the whole pack of you!" And these are his last words; the feeble effort of the Duke, "Pursue him and entreat him to a peace," we know must be fruitless. Thus even *Twelfth Night* ends as all but a tragedy. Yet how could Shakespeare help it? He knew—he had entered into—the enormous pride of Malvolio; and he knew that *nothing* could heal the hideous wounds that pride had suffered: Malvolio the man was more to him than Malvolio the "nayword"; and hence that despairing cry, which spoils the play but is justified of outraged human nature.

But, of all the "collaborators" of this kind, much the most important is Plutarch. Even Holinshed must yield to him. So far as we can judge, Plutarch was the writer whom Shakespeare knew best, loved most, and used with the most respect. He had, in the words of Macaulay, "thumbed his translation of Plutarch to rags." From that translation—the famous work of Sir Thomas North—he obtained materials for *Coriolanus*, *Julius Caesar*, and *Antony and Cleopatra*, as well as hints for *Timon of Athens*, the *Midsummer Night's Dream*, and possibly the *Two Noble Kinsmen*. In certain cases, as for example in large passages of *Coriolanus*, he often did little more than turn North's prose into verse. It is practically certain that in these plays he worked with the book not merely in his mind, but open before him. Here, then, we are on comparatively safe ground. If Shakespeare alters Plutarch, he does so (a few trifling errors apart) for a reason; but where he has left him unchanged no one can affirm dogmatically that he has always done so of set purpose. Thus, for instance, when in *Julius Caesar* he transforms "Phaonius the friend of Cato" into a bedlam poet or jigging fool, and alters the time of his intrusion upon the quarrel of Brutus and Cassius, it is the plain duty of the critic to seek for the reason of the change. On the other hand, when Brutus says that he has letters speaking of the murder of seventy senators by the triumvirs, "Cicero being one," this is a mere accident[1]. For the reason why Cicero's death is mentioned by Plutarch is to lead up to the death of Caius Antonius, whom Brutus executed in revenge for the murder of Cicero. But Shakespeare, in whose hands Brutus had grown into a man absolutely incapable of a revengeful murder, was obviously forced to omit the death of Antonius, forgetting meanwhile to excise the death of Cicero which had led up to it. A phrase intelligible enough in Plutarch thus becomes meaningless in Shakespeare: and it is a waste of time to seek for subtle intentions in the employment of it. Whether, again, Shakespeare meant Brutus, as it is so often said that he meant him, for a type of the unpractical philosopher who fails when he meddles

---

[1] I have noted this more fully elsewhere (*Suggestions*, III, p. 37).

with politics, can only be decided by a careful comparison with Plutarch, and especially by noting the alterations the poet has made. In our view, which we give with some hesitation, such a comparison will cast a doubt upon the current opinion. Similarly, in *Coriolanus*, the play which follows Plutarch more closely than any other, the *changes* in the character and actions of Menenius will probably be found to be very significant, while on the other hand it is not unlikely that the student will see reason to doubt the opinion held by many as to Shakespeare's hostile attitude to the tribunes and the common people. In *Antony and Cleopatra* faithfulness to Plutarch has even spoiled the symmetry of the play; a comparatively large number of scenes being apparently inserted merely because Plutarch had enlarged upon the incidents with which they have to do.

Many other points, as we have hinted, may be explained by considerations still more extraneous to literary aims. Some songs, we have no doubt, were inserted because there was a good boy singer in the cast: and some girls masqueraded as boys for an allied reason. Many of the farcical scenes, some of which are intruded at perhaps unfortunate moments, may have been due simply to the necessity of placating either the audience or the comic actor. Rather than permit the clown to say more than was set down for him in one place, Shakespeare may well have set down for him in another more than in his heart of hearts he wished him to say. The extraordinary number of battle-scenes—nearly all of which, probably, the modern hearer secretly wishes away—is almost certainly due to the popularity of such scenes in Elizabethan days: the audience dearly loved a good set-to, whether between Macbeth and Macduff or between two mighty monarchies like France and England; and Shakespeare was not the man to disappoint them, even though he thus diminished the poetry and the psychology in which he himself delighted. Again, the nature of his stage may have determined some of his work. Mr Walkley has rightly warned us never to forget the "apron"—that part of the stage which projected into the main body of the theatre like the handle of a fire-shovel, and —till Rich shortened it—served as a sort of rostrum for the protagonist. From it the actor, whether Hamlet or the clown, could address the audience like the chief of a Greek chorus delivering his "parabasis": hence doubtless the length of many of the soliloquies, in some of which the speaker forgets himself altogether, and declaims on general subjects, very eloquently it is true, but with small dramatic relevance. Such a soliloquy is "To be or not to be" —perhaps the most famous speech in English drama, though by no means throughout appropriate to the position in which Hamlet finds himself. To search such a speech with a view to elucidating the character of Hamlet, is like analysing some of the philosophic disquisitions in Euripides in order to discover the ideas of their supposed speakers. When Phaedra, for example, refutes the Socratic doctrine that virtue consists in knowledge (*Hippolytus*, 378), it is not Phaedra but Euripides that speaks: and when Hamlet talks of the insolence of office or the oppressor's wrong, the real voice belongs not to Hamlet but to the Shakespeare of the Sonnets. Again, when Oberon or Theseus makes a flattering reference to Queen Elizabeth, or some other *dramatis persona* discourses on the laws of acting, we must not confuse the puppet nominally expressing the views with the living man that pulls the strings. Euripides will here also supply the example and the warning. In the *Suppliants* (861) he ascribes to Adrastus a glowing eulogy upon Capaneus. But the eulogy is no guide to the character either of the praiser or of the praised; for, as we happen to know, the speech is a panegyric, not of the reckless blasphemer of the gods, but of their too careful worshipper, the blameless and unfortunate Nicias. But what if we do *not* happen to know? Both in Shakespeare and in the Greek dramatists there may be scores of such topical and personal allusions, which we miss for want of knowledge, and on which we build theories as baseless as the visionary palaces of Prospero. It may be that some of Falstaff is the real property of Chettle—if Chettle was in truth the groundwork of the character. It may be that some sayings of Fluellen would never have been uttered unless Roger Williams had uttered them before him—if it be true, as Dr Dover Wilson has plausibly suggested, that Williams was Fluellen's original. Even in Shylock there may be touches that belong rather to Lopez of London than to the usurer of Venice. In the Porter's reference to an "equivocator" we see the allusion to Garnet; but what of innumerable places where we do *not* see? It is pretty plain that the "Lady of the Strachey" of *Twelfth Night* is a topical allusion to some female Cophetua of the time; and Sir Toby's talk of the "undertaker" had probably a similar point. So, too, the "Deformed" of *Much Ado* must have referred to some actual character of the time who bore that nickname; and the "Humphrey Hour" of *Richard III*, though dead to us, was alive to the audience. Here, it is true, we can perceive that there *is* an allusion, if nothing more; but in many cases we can perceive nothing but a staring irrelevance, and often perhaps not even that[1].

To sum up in a word, the motto of the Shakespearean critic must be the opposite of the Danton-

---

[1] A parallel may be found in Macaulay. In his *Essay on Clive*, remarking that "ordinary criminal justice knows nothing of set-off," he adds as an illustration, "If a man has harnessed a Newfoundland dog to his little child's carriage, it is no defence that he was wounded at Waterloo." Who does not see that a case like this must have been before the courts in 1839, and must have been fresh in the memories of Macaulay's readers? Otherwise it is entirely without point. Perhaps someone may be more successful than I have been in tracing the case in the Law Reports of the time.

esque war-cry. Instead of "De l'audace, toujours de l'audace," he must study caution, caution, and evermore caution; for in plays in which the very stage directions are often most uncertain, there is little indeed of which we can be sure; and the wisest man in Shakespearean knowledge, like the wisest man in Greece, will not seldom prove to be he who knows best that he knows nothing.

iii

ἢ λέγε τι σιγῆς κρεῖττον, ἢ σιγὴν ἔχε. EURIPIDES.

THE highest thoughts, the deepest feelings, are
those for which no words can be found. The stars
are eternally meditating on the glory and handiwork
of God; yet, so the Psalmist assures us, they have no
speech nor language; their voice is not heard. And
so with our puny selves. Who can find phrases for
the emotions stirred in him by listening to the Ninth
Symphony, or who, watching the sea as it breaks
at the foot of the crags, does not echo the confession
of the poet, that his tongue cannot utter the thoughts
that arise in him? St Paul, awaking from his beatific
vision, refrained from telling what he had seen, not
only because it was unlawful, but because it was
impossible. How often have we not all felt, in our
little measure, what Wordsworth felt in his "high
hour of visitation," the sense of communion with
things so wonderful that even thought is not? Our
lighter feelings we may perhaps describe; our noblest
or our deepest, never. Perfect joy is always "perplexed for utterance," and perfect grief is dumb.
When Saturn wakes, in his shady vale, to the overwhelming realisation of lost dominion, he sits tranced
into the silence of a stone. When we, like ancient
Israel, are confronted with some tremendous and

decisive choice, we, like ancient Israel, "answer not a word," for all words are unequal to the magnitude of such a crisis.

Poets, it is true, whose business it is to express emotion, even the keenest, through a verbal medium, often attempt by turns of metaphor and simile or other indirections to compel words into an unnatural mould, and force them to strive after an unattainable end. As a painter represents grief or joy by the face, or a sculptor by an attitude, so a poet, who has scarcely any other means than words, tries to convey in words what can adequately be conveyed only by silence. Thus Milton, describing the agony of our first parents when aroused from their dream of false bliss, does, indeed, tell us that:

> Silent, and in face
> Confounded, long they sat, as strucken mute:

and, when Satan beholds the fellows of his crime, he remains long unable to speak: but, obedient to the laws of art, the poet, after a pause, gives both to Adam and to his great enemy words for their emotions. We may be sure that the silence was in the reality longer than it is in the description, and the speech, when it did come, more "constrained" and more broken than it is in the poet's translation of it. And so when the poet's vision is of things yet deeper than grief. Dante, for example, strains his mighty powers to describe the glories of heaven and

the rapture of the blessed, and all but succeeds.
Mystics like Blake and Boehme have tortured words
into a kind of ecstasy in order to make us see what
they see. But the *dramatic* poet, though he also
often makes his effort when it is certain the character
he represents would have been content with the
unspoken feeling, yet from time to time perceives
that the boldest metaphor, the loftiest rhyme, is
totally inadequate, and lets his heroes speak by
silence. In his desire to make all clear to his hearers,
he may say what would never have been said; but
now and then he wisely refrains. And it is remarkable that the poets who have oftenest thus refrained
from words are precisely those whose power of
verbal expression is such that one might think
nothing was beyond them. But they, better than
others, know the limitations of speech; and, though
they speak as no other men speak, are silent when
they reach the point beyond which speech would
fail. Employing as it were a sublime aposiopesis,
they stop short. Like Moses when contemplating
the infinite mercy of Jehovah, they say, "And now,
if thou wilt forgive their sin——" and add not a
word. It is with a few of these silences that I propose
to deal in this short paper.

Perhaps the sublimest work in the world is the
Book of Job; and to my mind the most impressive
passage in that most impressive poem is the one
which describes how the three friends lifted up their

eyes from afar off and knew him not; wherefore they sat down with him upon the ground in majestic Oriental sorrow for seven days and seven nights, and none spake a word, for they saw that his grief was very great. Not till the seven days and nights were past did Job open his mouth, and, with deliberation informing his intolerable agony, utter the passionate yet measured curse against his day. What thoughts must have passed through his mind during those long speechless hours!

In the Icelandic Kristni Saga we are told that at the great and decisive debate as to whether Christianity should be recognised or not, when things had come to such a pass that the country seemed likely to be split into two opposing factions, the Lawman Thorgeirr "laid him down in the sight of all, and spread a cloak over his head, and lay thus the whole day and all night, and the next day till the same hour." This symbolic silence calmed the warring chiefs, and brought peace into the assembly: the next day Thorgeirr rose, and summoned all men to the Hill of Laws, where he gave his decision, to which they all hearkened. But had he not been silent, they would have refused to listen when he spoke.

Discovering then, perhaps by actual experience, the dramatic value of silence, the greatest writers have, as we said, availed themselves of it. Even a Shakespeare, at certain crises, has felt that he has no words which can express the situation as forcibly as none at all. He knows, for instance, that while Regan and Goneril can be voluble enough about their "affection" for their father, Cordelia can only love and *be silent*: and he knows that other emotions, if as strong as Cordelia's love, must be silent too; and therefore, more than once or twice, he "commits" the expression of such emotions to "waste blanks." It is for the actors and the readers to lend these blanks the meaning with which the poet intended to charge them. We know that Aeschylus, also, was partial to this kind of speechless eloquence; and unfortunately not always, possibly in part through some failure of the actors, did it gain due appreciation from the audience. The Medicean *Life* tells us that in the *Niobe*, through two whole acts, the heroine sat by the tomb of her children, with her head muffled, uttering not a word; and in the *Ransom of Hector* Achilles, after a line or two addressed to Hermes, sat similarly muffled. It is clear that this bewildered the audience; and the biographer himself is of opinion that it was unintelligible and uninteresting. Nay, even Aristophanes, though an ardent admirer of Aeschylus, seems to have been fretted by it. We may well believe, indeed, that with nothing better than masked and buskined figures through which to work, Aeschylus was straining the resources of his art beyond their capacity: and the regular presence of a κωφὸν πρόσωπον, whose business it was to say nothing, and to which the audience was accustomed to pay little attention, may have hampered him yet further; for the audience may have been unable to tell at a glance which was the protagonist and which the speechless gesticulator with whom they were familiar. Yet it is probable that such scenes would have produced their full effect upon a people less given to the vocal expression of emotion than the Athenians. Had they, for instance, been performed before Arabs or Norsemen, they would have been duly appreciated.

But in one or two scenes, which have fortunately come down to us in full, Aeschylus achieved, and still achieves, an undoubted and a memorable triumph. In the first of these, be it noted, he ascribes this silent endurance to a supernatural being, and in the second to one who, though human, is yet inspired. But the strangeness to the Athenians would hardly be mitigated thereby; the examples of Ares and Aphrodite in the *Iliad* are not the only ones that might be adduced to show that to the Greeks a stoical impassiveness in their gods would seem as remarkable as in themselves; and the effect of these scenes, whether in the way of repugnance or in that of admiration, must have been very great. In any case we may well believe that no writer before Aeschylus would have thus ventured. When the two monstrous demons, with the reluctant Hephaestus in their train, arrive at the trackless and ultimate deserts of Scythia, to perform their dread task, it is

Kratos and Hephaestus who speak: the victim utters no sound. The horrible crucifixion is carried through; we hear the reverberation of the hammers and the clanking of the chains; from the "Awful Sufferer" we hear nothing. Hephaestus sighs over the agony he is constrained to inflict upon a kindred god: "Ay me, Prometheus, I grieve for thy woes; unwilling shall I nail thee, unwilling also, in indissoluble chains to this man-shunned crag": but Prometheus does not answer. Finally the savage Kratos gives vent to a parting taunt: "Falsely do the gods call thee the Far-sighted One; much foresight, methinks, wilt thou need to loose thyself from bonds like these"; but to taunt, as to compassion, the Titan is dumb. Not till the sound of the footsteps has died away in the distance does he break out into his cry to the divine aether and the swift-winged winds to look upon his pain. To us this silence has always seemed one of the sublimest things in literature: it is as if we were watching, in very truth, something more than human. It is like the vision of Eliphaz: "A Spirit passed before my face; it stood still but I could not discern the appearance thereof: *silence, and I heard a voice.*" Yet we must not forget that the Greek audience would *expect* a cry like that of Ajax, and would wonder why the chief actor remained as dumb as Bia. Only later would they, perhaps unwillingly, confess that the poet had done right to disappoint them.

Almost as lofty as this, and even more overwhelming as more pathetic, is the silence of Cassandra in the *Agamemnon*. Arriving with the King in the chariot, and fully conscious of the doom that awaits both him and her within the walls of the palace, she stands like a prophetic statue, motionless and tongueless. Yet from her very stillness there passes into the Chorus, and thence into the spectators, a horror of great darkness, so that they "mutter dimly, vexed in soul, and naught expecting ever to unfold from a breast on fire." To the mockings of Clytemnestra she answers nothing, hardly indeed seeming to hear the words; "her mood is as of a newly taken wild beast, as yet unused to captivity." When the queen has departed in anger, and not till then, she starts from her trance, and, scenting the yet unshed blood within the house, pours forth a torrent of foreboding words in which the coming tragedy, though described in dim prophetic imagery, is all too clearly revealed.

There is no scene in Shakespeare that calls for a silence so sublime as these. He moves more closely to the earth than Aeschylus, and we must not expect from him, in this sphere, flights quite so daring. Yet more than once he avails himself of the chance, when it offers, of avoiding words; and perhaps, as we have hinted above, the more visible play of his actors' features gives him certain advantages, *on the stage*, over Aeschylus; nor, of course, has he to contend with the confusion that might be caused by the presence of a *persona muta*. But his characters are on a less lofty plane than those of his great predecessor; and, as silence is the special language of the starry gods, he found fewer opportunities, among his very human kings and princes, for the use of this divine dialect. On one occasion, indeed, in his prentice days, he made a conspicuous failure. The silence of Silvia, in the *Two Gentlemen of Verona*, is not only gratuitous but stupid. But later he learned his art; and, as Macaulay pointed out, the silence of Hamlet in the first court-scene, though not equal to that of Prometheus, is yet very fine. The King opens with a long address, explaining his marriage to the Queen, and dilating on the conflict in his mind between grief for his brother's death and the sense of duty to his kingdom. As he speaks, we watch on Hamlet's face the emotions—loathing, contempt, disgust, doubt—all clearly written for us to see. The King then turns to Laertes, and, learning his desire to go to France, gives him permission. Hamlet's face now expresses a kind of scornful envy of the young man, who for trivial reasons can leave a court for which he is fitted, but in which the Prince, despite his hatred of it, is compelled to remain. Yet he utters no word; and even when Claudius directly speaks to him, his first speech is an "aside"—that is, not a speech but a thought: and his answer, when he is at last compelled to speak, is of the briefest. This is, indeed, "fine"; and it is the actor's business to make it finer still.

Of a slighter and more obvious kind is the silence of Macduff when he hears that his wife and children have been murdered. Unfortunately the scene in which this occurs is one of the dullest and feeblest in the whole of Shakespeare's works; and we cannot be sure that, if Shakespeare had been in a more inspired mood when he wrote it, he would not have made it more impressive. The effect is almost ruined by Malcolm's amazing tactlessness and want of sympathy: so much so, indeed, that our indignation against the Prince almost drowns our feeling for the bereaved father. Shakespeare well knew that sorrow like that has no words; and we can hardly believe that, at his best, he would have allowed Malcolm to wring words from a sufferer to whom silence is the only possible consolation. We are reminded, in a fashion, of the garrulous little maid in *Guinevere*, who, like many another babbler, harmed where she would heal: the Queen, bowed down upon her hands, silent, is thinking of her sins and their results, when the little maid, who brooks no silence, breaks it and enhances the misery.

More moving is another silence in the same play. When the mirth has been displaced, and the good meeting broken by Macbeth's "admired disorder," when the guests have all departed, and the ghost itself no longer threatens to return, Lady Macbeth, realising her shattered hopes and the crash of all her illusions, sits on, herself shattered, an image of stone, for what to the audience seems hours, and what is, in "reality," half the night. Macbeth himself strides restlessly to and fro; she moves no muscle, and appears hardly to breathe. It is a stillness that forebodes the coming quiet of the tomb. At length it is broken. "What is the night?" asks the husband; and the answer comes, as if a corpse had spoken, brief, monotonous, and hollow like a ghost's. "Almost at odds with morning, which is which": as her life is thenceforward to be at odds with dissolution. Six more brief words are spoken, and then, in "You lack the season of all natures, sleep," she utters the last waking words that ever leave her lips. To "sleep" the pair go off; but for her it is a sleep in which the past is always re-enacted, and from which the waking is to be an eternal slumber. That long silence, followed by a score of words, is one of the most penetrating effects that Shakespeare ever achieved.

When we turn to the quite different silence of Hermione at the end of *A Winter's Tale*, the parallel is rather with Euripides than with Aeschylus. This is a silence which, as far as Leontes is concerned, has already lasted sixteen years: and it is only right that she should remain upon her pedestal, voiceless and moveless, a little longer. It is right also—so intolerable is the wrong done to her—that though she submits to the embrace of her husband, and even, perhaps, embraces him in return, she should yet have no words for him. When she does speak, it is to Perdita alone, for whose sake only she has forced herself to live. Nothing could more eloquently declare the judgment of the poet on the poor creature whose crime, though forgiven, could never be forgotten. It may be—but a decision in this case is somewhat difficult—that the similar silence of Alcestis on her return from the grave marks in like fashion the judgment of Euripides on the conduct of Admetus, a husband whose selfishness, justly pilloried by his father, is nearly as bad as the insane suspicion of Leontes. It is true that Heracles ascribes the silence to a religious motive: "'Tis not permitted thee to hear word of hers until her consecration to the gods of death has been loosed, and until the third day dawns"; but Euripides was quite capable of introducing such a scruple for the sake of his orthodox hearers, while meaning something altogether different for the "intelligent" to whom he really addressed himself. Far more than Pindar, Euripides spoke words φωνᾶντα συνετοῖσιν. At any rate, whatever be the poet's true motive, the silence is far more vocal than any speech could have been[1].

[1] It is hardly necessary to do more than allude to the silence of Iphigeneia at her sacrifice, when, says Aeschylus (*Agamemnon*, 233), she lay "as in a picture," ὡς ἐν γραφαῖς. The poet tells us she wished, or tried, to speak, προσεννέπειν θέλουσα. But the speechless anguish of Agamemnon in the *Iphigeneia in Aulis*, where the author makes him veil his face to hide his tears (*Iph. Aul.* 1550), δάκρυα προῆγεν ὀμμάτων πέπλον προθείς, is said to have suggested to Timanthes his

Equally noteworthy, though conveying a very different significance, is the silence of Iago when his villainy has at last been revealed. He has, in a sense, achieved his aim; Othello has been ruined and Desdemona killed, but through the action of a being whom he had despised too utterly to take into account, he has failed to secure his own safety. As Bradley says, he had never meant his plot to be dangerous to himself; and, even when it proved to be so, he fancied that, his secret being shared with his wife alone, whose character he was convinced he knew, he was still safe. But when it dawns on him that the despised creature, in her love for her mistress, means to betray him, he is moved to anger, it is true, and to utter astonishment, but also to self-contempt. He is struck, like Achilles, in the one place where he is vulnerable; his intellectual pride is shattered. He, who thought he knew human nature through and through, has been mistaken as to the person he ought to have known best. He is not, as Bradley truly says, of a supremely intellectual type; but it has been his "grounds of faith" that he is so; he is as firmly convinced of his mental greatness as ever Malvolio of his repute; and the realisation that he, Iago, has made this clumsy blunder, has become the "geck and gull" of his own wife, is a tremendous blow to his self-esteem. He feels, we need not say,

famous veiled figure in his painting of the sacrifice. Whether this part of the play is by Euripides or another is, I believe, doubtful.

no remorse. But he does feel self-disgust, sudden, intense, overwhelming—and "From this time forth I never will speak word." That he will keep his vow we may be sure, despite the tortures with which Gratiano threatens him. To exhibit on his face the thoughts which chase themselves through his mind, "more fell than anguish, hunger, or the sea," is the actor's task; and an almost superhuman task it is.

There are two, or perhaps more, occasions on which this silence occurs in the extant plays of Sophocles, and in each case, by the mouth of the Chorus, the poet draws attention to it. It is perhaps by this simple device of a chorus-speech that Sophocles avoids the failure, if such it can be called, of Aeschylus: for we do not hear that in *his* case the audience complained of unintelligibility. In that terrible scene of *Oedipus the King*, in which Jocasta learns the full horror of her position, she does indeed speak, but it is to say that she will never speak again; and immediately she rushes out to seek in death a release from her agony. The Chorus then says, "Wherefore has she gone, O Oedipus? I fear that *from this silence* evils may break forth!" Similar is the case of Haemon in the *Antigone*: when his father has sentenced Antigone to death, even in the bridegroom's presence, the young man cries:

> Nay, not in my sight! Never dream thou this!
> Nor near me shall she die! Nowhere on earth
> Thou with thine eyes again shall see my face;

and the Chorus again emphasise the words:

> The man, O King, in wrath hath rushed away:
> Young hearts like his in pain wax desperate.

In each of these cases the doomed one rushes out to silence after a speech of his own; but in the two following he listens, without a word, to a long speech of another, and *then* goes forth; a situation more strictly parallel to those we have considered above. Somewhat later, in this very play of *Antigone*, Haemon's mother Eurydice listens in speechless anguish to the Messenger's long story of her son's death. The Prince has gone to the inmost recesses of Antigone's tomb, and like Romeo bewailing Juliet has clasped her waist and sorrowed for his bridal's ruin, lost in Hades.

> Then that ill-starred one,
> Wroth with himself, plunged then and there the blade
> Deep in his own side; and, ere sense had swooned,
> Embraced the maiden with his failing arm:
> And, gasping out the last sharp gust of breath,
> Dashed with the bloody spray her pallid face.
> Clasping a corpse, a corpse he lies: in halls
> Of Hades is his bridal consummated.

To all this the mother listens speechless; not till the last word is uttered does she rush out: and here again the poet is ready with his explanatory chorus:

> What would'st thou guess from this? The queen is passed
> From sight again, naught saying, good or ill.

Messenger.

> Yea, I too marvel: yet I feed on hope
> She means to stir her maidens to the keening:
> Not void of wit is she, that she should err.

Chorus.

> I know not. Ominous this silence more
> To me than had she uttered bitter cry.

Very similar is the scene in the *Trachiniae*, where Deianeira hears from Hyllus the dreadful story of the death of the hero she loves, and by her own fatal error: a story ending in a terrible denunciation. "May the wrathful Erinys take vengeance on thee! 'Tis lawful that thus I pray, for thou art no more my mother, and hast cast away, thyself, all mother's claims." Once more the Chorus:

> Why dost thou part in silence? Seest thou not
> That silence speaks thee conscious of thy guilt?

We see thus that Sophocles, though so great, was less far removed from his audience than Aeschylus; with all his genius he was a typical Athenian, and understood what Athenians required. Even when he did not give them the vocal sorrow which they expected, he told them why he refused it, and saw to it that they understood.

Far finer, to our mind, than any of these Sophoclean silences is that of Phaedra in the *Hippolytus* of Euripides, which, it is worth while to observe, is due to a deliberate afterthought. As Professor Gilbert

Murray points out, in the first recension of the play Phaedra actually declared her love; and this more obvious treatment of the theme was preferred by both Seneca and Racine. "But Euripides in his second thoughts reached a far more austere and beautiful effect: his Phaedra goes to her death without having spoken one word to Hippolytus; she has heard him but has not answered." This is still more noteworthy in that Euripides, like Sophocles, well knew that his countrymen liked to bewail their griefs aloud, and in one of his lost plays made a speaker say, like Malcolm, that sorrow should have words. But here he gives his hearers not what they wanted, but what he himself felt that nature demanded. When the nurse has betrayed the fatal secret, the Queen tells the Chorus:

> No way I know but one, to die with speed——
> Sole cure for these my woes:

but before she can depart, Hippolytus bursts in, furiously upbraiding the nurse, and not sparing Phaedra herself. To all his words Phaedra listens, but says nothing. There is, indeed, nothing that words *can* say. When Hippolytus has departed, but not till then, she pours out her feelings to the impersonal chorus: which is like Prometheus telling his woes to the deaf winds and the dumb air.

I need hardly adduce more of these instances[1].

---

[1] Before leaving Greek plays, however, we may notice an effect very similar to silence—that gained by the *absence* of Ajax and of Philoctetes

But I must for a moment dwell on one, the most impressive of all, which is to be found as the climax of every Shakespearean tragedy, more speaking than the long harangues of the *Deus ex machina* which close so many Greek plays—the silence of death. When all has been said that can be said, and when our feelings are too painfully harrowed for utterance, that Silence descends upon the scene, and fitly closes all. When utter and crushing sorrow has finally dumbed even the eloquence of Lear, when the dagger of Othello has reconciled him to the world and re-united him to Desdemona, when Brutus has at last made peace with the ghost of Caesar, when Cleopatra has rejoined Antony, we want no more words. A few obituary lines may be recited by survivors; an epitaph may be read over Coriolanus, or a triumphant paean sung over Macbeth; but it is the corpses that actually speak to us, like Abel, after death. What we, the hearers and readers, are feeling, can be rightly spoken by no living tongue, nor can the poet, however eloquent, add anything by means of words. Every Elizabethan tragedy really ends with the last words of Hamlet, "The rest is silence."

while the respective pairs of plotters speak outside. Both heroes have been silent long and we recognise that they are silent still; although they are not visible on the stage to make their dumbness vocal.

iv

THE TRANSLATION OF THE NEW TESTAMENT

Touching translations of holy Scripture, albeit we may not disallow of their painful travels herein who strictly have tied themselves to the very original letter; yet the judgment of the Church, as we see by the practice of all nations, Greeks, Latins, Persians, Syrians, Aethiopians, Arabians, hath been ever, that the fittest for public audience are such, as following a middle course between the rigour of literal translators, and the liberty of paraphrasts, do with greatest shortness and plainness deliver the meaning of the Holy Ghost. Which being a labour of so great difficulty, the exact performance thereof we may rather wish than look for.   HOOKER, *Ecclesiastical Polity*, Book v, 19.

Non converti ut interpres, sed ut orator: non verbum pro verbo necesse habui reddere, sed genus omnium verborum vimque servavi; non enim ea me adnumerare lectori putavi oportere, sed tanquam adpendere.   CICERO on his translation of DEMOSTHENES.

THE problem of providing a satisfactory English New Testament is by no means solved. There is, indeed, no agreement as to the principles on which such a work should be based; and still less, if less than none be possible, as to the merits of the versions already before the public. The Revised Version of 1881, like most human productions, failed to please everybody. It was attacked from the most diverse quarters and on the most various grounds; for choosing the wrong text to translate, and for translating it badly; for false Greek and for false English; for putting the correct version into the margin and for putting into the text what ought to have been in the margin; for a hundred other reasons, some serious, some trivial. As a result, at first its chances of acceptance were slight. Dean Burgon, as is well known, went to his grave with the proud conviction that he had killed the Revised Version. Many others, however, were unwilling to allow Burgon the sole glory, and insisted on a recognition of their own share in the murder.

After forty years, perhaps, one may survey the field of battle with calmer eyes, and take a juster view of the results than the combatants themselves. It is now evident that whatever may be the fate of the Revised Version, whether it is to die or whether it is to live, it was not killed by Dean Burgon. In the first place, it is not yet dead at all: for it still sells; and most books are not like Indians, that sell better when they are dead. In the second place, it is precisely where Burgon's attacks were keenest that time has proved the Version strongest. Objection may be taken here and there to readings preferred by Westcott and Hort, on whose text the Version (to speak in general terms) was based. Those two great scholars may perhaps have been too uncompromising in their idolatry of the Vatican manuscript; and future research will probably redress the balance slightly in favour of other traditions[1]. But that the principles of Burgon will ever

---

[1] Personally, I believe that in *Acts*, at least, there will be more consideration given to the "Western Text."

prevail, that the Received Text (for this is what his views amount to) will ever be received again, is inconceivable. As well expect Travis to be preferred to Porson, and the Three Witnesses to come to life again, as expect Burgon's criticisms on the Greek text adopted by the Revisers to regain credit. The final edition of the Greek Testament will not be that of Westcott and Hort. But it will differ from it only in minutiae; while it will be poles apart from that approved by Burgon.

The objections to the Revised Version that still hold their ground are of a different kind. Pedantic alterations in places where the translation was already sufficiently accurate; vexatious triflings with a time-honoured tradition; a want of feeling for harmony and rhythm; and in general a lack of proper respect for the noble Version they were set to revise and not to mangle—these are the crimes now laid to the charge of the men of 1881. Why, for example, people ask, should the same Greek word, regardless of the context, be always rendered by the same English word? Why should the Greek aorist, in defiance of English idiom, be so constantly rendered by the past indefinite, and that too when the Authorised Version has to be altered in order to consummate the outrage? Why, again, should the appearance of an article in the Greek be invariably signalised by the appearance of an article in English, whether the genius of our language requires it or not? In a word, the prevailing view to-day is that the Revised Version may do tolerably well as a "crib" for a schoolboy preparing his Westcott and Hort, but will most emphatically *not* suit the average English reader, who is irritated by it at every turn, and to irritate whom might almost seem to have been one of its main purposes.

Some of these charges, it is true, are scarcely worth refutation. Such is that which is based on the rejection of verse-divisions—a charge going back to the time when isolated texts, torn more or less violently from their surroundings, were regarded as individual wholes, to be misinterpreted accordingly. It is a charge unworthy of anyone with the slightest pretensions either to scholarship or to literary feeling—not that it has not been made by pretenders to both—and can emanate only from the dullest and most unreasoning conservatism. The charge of want of English, also, is rendered absurd when we reflect that the three chiefs of the modern school, who were supposed to have had most to do with the "pedantic" alterations, were also the three whose version of the Book of Wisdom is a confessed masterpiece, not only of Greek scholarship, but of English—strong, pure, harmonious, and undefiled. The Revisers may have been occasionally too exact for the beauty of their own language; but the reason was that they preferred accuracy to ornament: they *could* have written flowing English had they so chosen.

But the fact remains that this kind of irritation with the Revised Version, so far from diminishing with time, appears rather to increase. Hitherto, indeed, while the Version has on the whole gained and held favour in Nonconformist chapels, it has made virtually no progress in Anglican churches. A clergyman here and there may be found who substitutes a correction from the Revised Version for a mistaken rendering in the Authorised; but there are very few indeed, perhaps none, who habitually read whole lessons from the Revised. And this after forty years—a period amply sufficient for the disappearance of ordinary prejudice.

No one, then, can be surprised that a movement has been gaining strength in favour of a new revision of the Authorised Version; a revision confined—whether wisely or unwisely we shall consider later—to the removal of actual mistakes, and the substitution of intelligible words and phrases for such as are likely to be misunderstood. Such a revision would probably make only slight changes in the Revised Version of the Old Testament, which has roused but little antagonism. But it will, in the New, revert, as far as it possibly can without serious inaccuracy, to the version of three hundred years ago.

About twenty years since, a "corrected New Testament," fashioned on these lines, made its appearance and gained some favour; and shortly afterwards Dean Beeching, whose English scholarship has such just repute, wrote a series of articles pointing out what he regarded as needless alterations in the Revised Version, remarking on faults of idiom due to a too slavish adherence to the Greek, and suggesting a revision of the kind we have described. For example, he would, we fancy, go back to "For the Lord God *omnipotent* reigneth," in place of the irritating "almighty" of the Revisers; but on the other hand he would give us "For our *citizenship* is in heaven" instead of the misleading "conversation" of the Authorised Version—a rendering correct enough in 1611, but giving rise to-day to the most ludicrous misunderstandings. Similarly, doubtless, he would have given us "hinder" for "let," "condemn" for "damn," "cause to stumble" for "offend," and the like; nor will he follow the Authorised Version in its wanton confusion as to proper names. That such changes are absolutely necessary is, indeed, obvious: there are many hundreds of places in which the Authorised Version is incorrect, deceptive, inconsistent, or unintelligible; nor can any modern version, however conservative, avoid wholesale changes. If anyone doubts this, let him take up, for example, the Second Epistle to the Corinthians, and after reading it carefully through ask himself whether he thinks that the translators themselves always understood what they were writing. That the ordinary careless reader *thinks* he understands, is nothing to the point. We have seen many devout persons serenely edified by hearing "It shall be for those" (Isa. xxxv. 8), or "strain at a gnat" (Matt. xxiii. 24), or "All my springs are in thee" (Ps. lxxxvii. 7), read with a certain degree of unction; though it is needless to say that all these sentences are without meaning, and that the last one has been given up by Professor Cheyne himself[1]. On the other hand, the Dean and those who agree with him do not think the changes, numerous as they must be, will be anything like as frequent or as irritating as those made by the Revisers.

Moved by these ideas, a deputation some time since addressed the Archbishop of Canterbury, and put before him the case for a new Revised Version of this kind. The Archbishop, as becomes a metropolitan, was cautious in his reply; but he showed himself decidedly favourable. He suggested that experiments should be made along the proposed lines; that, for example, a translation of one of the more difficult books, such as the Epistle to the Hebrews, should be published, and that according to the reception given to it further experiments should be started. Since then his desire has, to a certain extent, been met: there has appeared the work by Sir Edward Clarke, containing the Epistles of St Paul treated in this manner. Sir Edward is not

---

[1] We have even known people wax enthusiastic over "He shall deliver the island of the innocent" (Job xxii. 30)—a ridiculous mistranslation.

only a great advocate, he is a devout Churchman; and his work is interesting as that of a man who represents, perhaps, the average of cultured lay opinion. He is, of course, strongly conservative in tendency; he actually preserves the ascription of the Epistle to the Hebrews to St Paul; and his work will, therefore, probably receive correction at the hands of his successors. But we are not likely, at present, to find a better example of the kind of work which seems adapted to satisfy the average opinion of the Church of England. His revision is meant either to be read in churches itself, or to lead the way to revisions which shall so be read; and we imagine that nothing markedly different from it will ever be so read, at least at Anglican services. And yet we confess we wish it were otherwise. While we yield to none in our admiration of the Authorised Version as a specimen of Jacobean, or, rather, early Tudor, English, we regard it as, for the purposes of the ordinary reader of to-day, a bad translation and a source of innumerable mistakes and misunderstandings. That, if it cannot cease to be read in churches, a better version, and a very different one, should be adopted for private reading and for family worship, we regard as certain. Such a paradoxical position as this, of course, requires defence; and the following pages will be devoted to defending it.

In the first place, the Authorised Version is a literal translation; and it may be laid down as a rule with hardly a single exception that a literal translation cannot be an exact one. Equivalence between one language and another, if to be found at all, is to be found in the mass and not in the detail, in the sentence (sometimes in the paragraph) and not in the word. Languages so different as English and Greek, in particular, do not admit of literal transfusion. A poem of Heine, or a page of simple Swedish, may, it is true, *sometimes* be rendered literally into English; but even in such cases the *feel* of one language can scarcely ever be given in the other except by considering sentences, or often blocks of sentences, as wholes rather than as aggregates of words [1]. Much more so in the case of Greek. Take any of the standard translations—Jowett's *Plato*, Butcher's *Poetics of Aristotle*, Jebb's *Sophocles*. Have any of these men—masters of both languages as they were—made the slightest attempt to attain literality? Have they not rather, from the very desire of precision, shunned literality like the plague? And has not their success in catching the meaning of their original—to say nothing of the transfusion of its spirit—been in inverse proportion to the closeness of their adherence to its letter? It is true, of course, that the Greek of the New Testament, being far simpler in construction and far less idiomatic than

---

[1] "Luther has lived himself into the original, in order not to render it literally, but to cast it freely, and in the deepest sense faithfully, into true German" (*Delitzsch on the Psalms*, Eng. trans. I. p. 63).

that of a Plato or a Sophocles, makes less demand on the subtler idioms of English; but the fact remains that the translators of 1611 have repeatedly failed, through literality, in expressing the meaning, when a greater degree of freedom would have enabled them to give it with fair exactness. An example, already adduced by Dr Weymouth in the preface to his *New Testament in Modern Speech*, will be sufficient to prove our case. In 2 Cor. x. 6, the Authorised Version reads, "And having in a readiness to revenge all disobedience, when your obedience is fulfilled"; a sentence which the scholar can only understand by thinking of the original—ἐν ἑτοίμῳ ἔχοντες—and which it is certain no ordinary English reader ever understood at all. How vastly more clear is the rendering of Weymouth: "While we hold ourselves in readiness to punish every act of disobedience, as soon as ever you as a church have fully shown your obedience": or that of the *Twentieth Century New Testament*: "We are fully prepared to punish every act of rebellion, when once your submission has been put beyond doubt." To multiply examples would be merely to darken counsel. But one might well wonder whether such passages as the following are intelligible without a commentary: "It is Corban, that is to say, a gift, by whatsoever thou mightest be profited by me" (Mark vii. 11); "Now faith is the substance [1] of things hoped for, the evidence of

---

[1] The real meaning of the word rendered "substance" is, as the study of the Papyri has shown, "fee-simple."

things not seen" (Heb. xi. 1); "But after their own lusts shall they heap to themselves teachers, having itching ears" (2 Tim. iv. 3); and a score of others. These, it may be mentioned, are passages tolerably plain in the original Greek; but, where the original is obscure, the translation is often still more so. Thus in Jude 23: "And others save with fear, pulling them out of the fire; hating even the garment spotted by the flesh," no light whatever is thrown upon the darkness by the translation.

Such literalism has its advantages; but not in a work intended to be heard in churches *without comment*, nor in a work intended to be read at home by pious persons who may not be able to afford exegetical books. The fact is that, in their reasonable dread of giving too much interpretation, the Authorised translators, and the Revisers after them, have often left the reader with hardly any clue to their meaning at all.

Such a statement it may be well to buttress not only by reason but by authority. It is satisfactory then to be able to quote the opinion of that great Greek scholar, W. G. Rutherford, as given in the preface to his translation of the Epistle to the Romans. After adducing a dozen examples of obscurity in the English due to excessive literality, he concludes:

Is it fair, I ask, to the English reader to translate such idioms word for word? A man cannot return to his place after reading a lesson to an ordinary congregation without feeling that to the bulk of his hearers it would have carried almost as much meaning if he had read it in Greek. Unhappily the time is still far distant when it will become possible to prepare some sort of authoritative Targum for the use of the laity.

But, grave as the fault of literality may be, a far more important objection to the Authorised Version, considered as a possession for the present day, remains to be made. Were all its actual errors corrected, were all its literalisms removed in favour of idiomatic renderings, there would yet be left the most serious defect of all. The Authorised Version is antiquated in style. It is probable that it always was so, for like its own successors it was intended to be not a new translation, but a revision of an older one. Based as it was on the Bishops' Bible of 1568, which itself was but a *rifacimento* of Tyndale's (1526), it perpetuated a style of writing which had already largely gone out of fashion. It would not be difficult, though it might be tedious, by instituting a comparison between the Authorised Version and contemporary prose works, to show that it was written with a *conscious* look backwards. Thus, for example, it is less pedantic but far more antique than the Douay Bible. But such a proof is beside our present point: what is relevant is that the book is *now* antiquated—a fact, of course, neither controverted nor controvertible. Most people, indeed, regard this characteristic as rather a merit than a blemish. The

Revisers of 1881 have deliberately retained this feature in their own work.

> In our sparing introduction of words not found in the Authorised Version we have usually satisfied ourselves that such words were employed by standard authors of nearly the same date, and had also that general hue which justified their introduction into a Version which has held the highest place in the classical literature of our language. We have never removed any archaisms, whether in structure or in words, except where we were persuaded either that the meaning of the words was not generally understood, or that the nature of the expression led to some misconception of the true sense of the passage.

So say the Revisers in their preface; and the truth of it is manifest. They have altered "secure" to "rid of care," and "let" to "hinder"; but they have kept the whole archaic colour of the old translation. Their rules, indeed, forbade them to change it; but it is plain they would have retained it even if no rules had been made. And it is just here that our main quarrel with them lies. Archaism is the unpardonable sin in a translation of the New Testament; *for there is nothing archaic in the original.*

There are, of course, some books which not only permit, but demand, translation in such a style. Few would deny that the best medium into which to render the *Odyssey* is language of this antiquated type: for, while to the author himself there was, in all probability, nothing strange about his diction, which was the natural poetic diction of his time, yet there must have been something quaint and curious about it to those Greeks—let us say of the age of Aristotle—whose general culture corresponded on the whole most nearly to our own. For this reason the style in question was adopted, with some skill and success, by Butcher and Lang in their version. Similarly, the *Bhagavad Gita*, the *Mabinogion*, and Snorri's *Edda* should be thus rendered; and large portions of the Old Testament are rightly thus translated, not only in the Authorised Version but in the Revised. No one, we trust, will ever try to tell the story of Joseph in the style of Meredith, or to "transprose" the little idyll of Ruth into a version like that of Harwood, with its simplicity and poetry driven out in favour of eighteenth-century "spirit and elegance." But everything depends on proportion. If the most varying styles are all rendered into this one style, the whole aim of translation is lost. That the peculiar character of these very episodes may be properly appreciated, their style must be markedly different from that of other works, nay, from that of other portions of the same book; precisely as, in Arnold's *History of Rome*, the manner in which Arnold gives the early legends differs from that in which he describes the campaigns of Hannibal. What would be the impression made on the reader's mind if Cannae were told in the same way as the battle of Lake Regillus? Yet, by a strange fate, it is the style appropriate to legend which has been adopted, by devout and believing Christians, as suitable for describing the life of Christ. Still worse, the profound and argumentative letters of Paul are rendered as nearly as possible into the same dialect, and the philosophical character of the Apostle's mind is thus hopelessly obscured.

True, if there were anything in the original to justify this treatment, if the style of the Greek was itself poetical or archaic, it would be necessary, in the interests of faithfulness, to reproduce that style to the best of our ability in our own language. But, if any certainty is ever to be attained about a dead language, it is indubitable that in the original Greek of the New Testament there is nothing of the kind. It is often very difficult to ascertain the precise effect a certain style had upon its first readers and the style which our translation is to use to produce a corresponding effect upon the readers to-day. Do the neat and regular elegiacs of Ovid, for example, correspond to the couplets of Pope, and those of Propertius to the looser metrical effects of Keats or of Morris? But even when this insoluble question is solved, there yet remains another. Was the Roman taste that preferred Ovid to Propertius as vitiated as that of our Augustan ancestors who preferred Pope to Spenser? If so, to translate Ovid *to-day* into Popian couplets may be passing a censure on him by the mere choice of a discredited style. In fact, a translation that suited its original two hundred years ago may be precisely the one most unsuitable nowadays. Again, what was the exact effect produced on contemporaries of Horace by his *Odes?* Was it in any way similar to that produced on us by the dainty and delicate, yet elaborate, poems of Mr William Watson? Is Virgil Miltonic, or is he Tennysonian? All these are questions that can never be answered, and that even if answered to-day will need another answer to-morrow. But in the case of the Greek of the New Testament, while an exact answer is, of course, unattainable, a tolerable approximation can be found with fair certainty. There is, for instance, nothing antiquated, nothing poetical, nothing even highly literary, about the style of Mark. That of Luke, says Alford, is the elegant language of a gentleman of education; not pedantically classical, but studious and elaborate in his sentences, and often complex in construction; while he is also capable of varying his style to suit his substance. But it is safe to say that, except when deliberately imitating the Septuagint or some other early work, he is no more archaistic than Bernard Shaw. With John's Gospel, again, the case is similar. John is unambitious, and never ventures into intricate sentences; and hence his style, though peculiar, is, as we know on the evidence of Dionysius of Alexandria, "smooth and free from error"; but John would not have avoided error if he had aimed, like Lucian, at imitating the style of Plato. The style of the Apocalypse, whoever was its author, is, by all competent testimony, "not completely Greek, full of foreign idioms, abrupt, and in places showing actual solecisms." All these are facts that admit of no denial; they are obvious to scholars to-day and asserted by Greeks of times near to that at which the New Testament was written. If any doubt existed twenty years ago, such doubt has been completely set at rest by the discovery of the Egyptian papyri, which have provided us with innumerable exemplars of every form of Greek style as it was in the first century. As far as we can know the *feel* of any ancient language, we know the feel of the Greek of the New Testament, and if anything is certain in this world it is that the New Testament, when written, was a *modern* book, striking its readers in a way totally different from that in which the Authorised Version strikes us. Its Greek, good, bad, or indifferent, narrative, hortatory, or reflective, was Greek of the day. Yet our Authorised Version, which Dr Beeching and Sir Edward Clarke would perpetuate, gives us always the English of three hundred years ago, if not that of a still earlier date. Nay it has, perhaps, an even worse defect. It gives us practically the same style for Matthew, Mark, Paul, Peter, and Luke; a style always and everywhere dignified, poetical, and archaic, removed equally from the matter-of-factness of the plain Mark and from the gentlemanly modernity of the cultured Luke; while the rude Greek of Revelation is represented by, perhaps, the loftiest English in the whole New Testament! This is not translation, it is sublimation, or rather, to speak plainly, falsification.

But for the blinding influence of custom, we should long ago have recognised the absurdity of such a state of affairs. There is no other book that ever has been, or ever will be, translated on such a principle; nor has the New Testament itself been thus treated in any other circumstances. No missionary, when trying to render the Bible into the language of his converts, searches for an antiquated dialect of that language, or for a form of it which must inevitably lead half his readers to misunderstand the character of the book[1]. Nor did previous English translators conceive such a fantastic idea. The Anglo-Saxon Version of the Gospels is by various hands and of various merit. It is too often defaced by close adherence to the original Latin; but it betrays not the slightest sign of a desire to use an English different from that of contemporary prose writers. It is, not unnaturally, inferior in purity and ease of flow to the translations scattered through the *Homilies* of Aelfric; but its aim is precisely the same as that of that great master of English—to render "in nostram *consuetam sermocinationem,* ob aedificationem *sim-*

[1] John Hunt, the apostle of Fiji, speaks of his determination to make his Fijian version of the N.T., as far as possible, *intelligible* to the natives, and quotes as his justification the passage of Hooker which I have prefixed to this essay.

plicium; ideoque," says Aelfric, "nec obscura posui-
mus verba, sed *simplicem Anglicam.* Nec ubique
transtulimus verbum ex verbo, sed sensum ex sensu."
The so-called Bible of Wyclif, again, though often
sadly inexact in point of scholarship, is written in
the pure English of its time, and (where the writer
understood it himself [1]) would have been easily
understood by its hearers—as, indeed, we have
observed it easily understood in a Yorkshire village
even to-day. But the Bible, as presented to King
James, is to go on conveying a false idea of its
original. Actual mistakes, it is true, are to be corrected; but the one great mistake, in comparison
with which all the others put together are as nothing,
is to remain. Nay, worse: it is to increase; for every
decade will make the Authorised Version more
antiquated, and thus widen the interval between its
tone and that of the original Greek.

But, cry the horrified conservatives, are you to
destroy the old familiar rhythm and balance? Most
certainly, when the old rhythm is not that of the
Greek, or when there is no rhythm at all in the
original to excuse its intrusion into the version.
Even in the translation of the poetry of the Old
Testament, the rhythm is often false. Hear what

---

[1] It is probable, to give one striking example, that he did not understand what was meant by "the wordis of hym that gaderith, of the sone
spuynge" (Proverbs xxx. 1), which appear in the A.V. as "the words
of Agur the son of Jakeh" (Vulgate, "Verba Congregantis filii
Vomentis").

Professor Cheyne says of the older versions of the Psalter:

> It is not just to these precious lyrics to read them exclusively in a version several centuries old. Exquisite as the Prayer Book version may be, and possibly the Bible version, too, to ears unfamiliar with the older music, either rendering does but convey that part of the meaning and the charm which was accessible to the men of the sixteenth century. The rhythmic effect of the old versions of the Bible (on which Matthew Arnold, in *Isaiah of Jerusalem*, lays so much stress), may be admirable of its kind, but it is not the lightning-like effect of the Hebrew; the collocations of words and syllables may be effective, but they are often very far away from the sense of the original (*The Book of Psalms Translated*, p. v).

If this is true of the poetical books, what of the epistles and narratives of the New Testament?

Beauty of rhythm is, indeed, largely a matter of imagination, or of personal taste. A child admires a lilting measure, though it occur in the midst of prose, while the mature ear rejects it with disgust. Often, the "rhythm" is merely another word for "familiarity." As Professor Cheyne hinted, in the passage just quoted, the "rhythms" of the Prayer Book version of the Psalms are usually preferred by Churchmen; those of the Authorised Version by Nonconformists of equal taste and culture: and the difference is due solely to the fact that Churchmen are familiar from their childhood with the one, and Nonconformists with the other. A glance at the suggestions of the American Revisers—men certainly not inferior to their English brethren in literary feeling—will provide other examples of the same truth.

There is in fact every reason to believe that the "beauty" of the Authorised Version is, to a greater extent than we imagine, the creation of our intimacy with it. It certainly did not strike its earliest readers, unused as they were to its "rhythms," as particularly wonderful. To prove this statement, we need go no further than the well-known passage in Selden's *Table Talk*. "There is no book so translated as the Bible"—and what Selden means by "so" we soon see.

> If I translate a French book into English, I turn it into English phrase, not into French English. I say 'tis cold, not it makes cold; but the Bible is rather translated into English words than into English phrase:—which is well enough so long as scholars have to do with it; but when it comes among the common people, Lord, what gear do they make of it!

What Selden is alluding to is such phraseology as "Holy of Holies," "Pharisee of the Pharisees": but it is noteworthy that these phrases, once utterly unidiomatic, have now, by familiarity, become part and parcel of the English language. Bad grammar, in fact, has become good by use. The same has been the case with the words of Daniel, "Ancient of Days," which simply mean "an old man": but which, by false association, have attained a sublimity totally unintended by the original writer: as, conversely, the parallel "infant of days" (Isa. lxv. 20) has *not* attained sublimity simply because it occurs in a less familiar passage. Sometimes, it is true, the translators have failed to foist a foreign idiom upon us, though they did their best. Thus, in the second Epistle to Timothy (i. 5) they give us, "The unfeigned faith which was in thy mother and thy grandmother, and I am persuaded *that* in thee also"; where even the Revisers have refused to follow them. Examples might be multiplied *ad libitum*; but these will be sufficient. As for want of precision, which has in very truth led the unlearned to make "sad gear," it is enough to refer to a single passage. What ordinary reader understands "A measure of wheat for a penny" (Rev. vi. 6), or perceives that the seer is proclaiming *not* pre-war cheapness, but a famine so severe that wheat is sold at twelve times its usual price? And yet our Revisers rejected the advice of their American brethren to render *denarius* or *drachma* not by "penny" but by "shilling"—a simple change which would have saved many a misunderstanding.

A little leaven leaveneth the whole lump; and the beauty of some parts of the Version has made many people imagine that the whole is beautiful. But in the work of forty-seven writers there *must* be degrees of merit: there may be degrees varying from the perfect to the bad: and nothing but slavish superstition would have prevented people from seeing that there are many bad verses, nay many bad chapters, in our Bible—and especially in the New Testament. And here, once more, we can add authority to reason. Coleridge is generally regarded as a good critic. Hear what he says (*Table Talk*, August 20, 1833):

> I think there is a perceptible difference in the elegance and correctness of the English in our versions of the Old and New Testaments. I cannot yield to the authority of many examples of usages which may be alleged from the New Testament version. St Paul is very often most inadequately rendered, and there are slovenly phrases which would never have come from Ben Jonson or any other good prose writer of that day.

That Coleridge is right anyone may assure himself if, laying aside prejudice, he will read through the epistle to which we have already referred—the second to the Corinthians.

Let us, however, assume for the sake of argument that the stylistic and rhythmical beauty of the Version is not the mere product of use and time, but corresponds to some "objective" reality: does it follow that it is correctly introduced when there is no such feature in the original? Too frequently that original has been doctored into a harmony that does not belong to it, as the "vulgarities" of Homer were doctored into elegance by Pope. We do not want our Bible without its warts.

One remembers, of course, the dictum of Archbishop Trench, that there ought to be a certain strangeness in our religious language, a certain distance from the common, as our ecclesiastical architecture differs, and ought to differ, from that of our dwelling-houses. Here speaks the Church dignitary who likes his clothing to mark him off from his fellow-men—at the cost of never knowing what his fellow-men think. To his doctrine we should agree so far, and only so far, as to admit that our religious language should be free from excessive colloquialism, meanness, loose grammar. Anything beyond this savours of superstition, and tends to foster that most pernicious of beliefs, that sanctity is something apart from common life. A halo round the head of a saint, in a medieval picture, may have worth as symbolism; but if taken literally is dangerous. We shall never understand true saintliness until we realise that a saint, in external circumstances and appearance, is indistinguishable from other men. The life of our Lord Himself loses half its significance if we do not see, and continually constrain ourselves not to forget, that to outward view it went on like that of other poor carpenters, and that, if He came to-day, He would wear the garb, and speak the language, of an ordinary artisan. What He came to show, among other things, was just this, that the holiest of lives may be led by the most commonplace of men; that there needs no Stoic aloofness, no Epicurean ease of circumstances, to make the holy man. His divinity moved to and fro, visible indeed to the pure and to the penitent, but invisible to the worldly, who could not understand how a mere carpenter, the son of Joseph, with brothers and sisters like others, the denizen of a town from which proverbially no good came, could claim to be a Son of God. This deadly heresy, no less common in England than in Judaea, that the kingdom of heaven comes "with observation," was what He went about to combat; and it is our business to-day to beat it down by every lawful means. The Son of Man came eating and drinking, speaking the plain language of His time, dressed like the men of His time: let us do nothing to dim the plain reality of the picture.

What the halo is to the saint of medieval art, that the dialect of the Authorised Version is to the literary aspect of religion: it hides from us the actuality of Christ, the humanity of His apostles, and the holy commonness of their daily lives. To prove this, it is sufficient to compare the Gospel of Mark in the version of 1611 with that in the *Twentieth Century New Testament.*

To retain the phraseology of the Authorised Version, then, is not merely a piece of archaistic pedantry, like that which led Charles Fox to exclude from his *History* all words that had not the sanction of Dryden. It is to run a serious risk of throwing the life of Christ into the realm of dreamland. Told in a style which recalls that of Malory, it tends to give the impression that Nathanael is no more real than

Sir Bors, that the Woman of Samaria is as phantasmal as Guinevere, and that the "Good News" was proclaimed by its earliest teachers in a dead jargon no more significant than that of chivalry is to us. When the Apostles looked round for words in which to clothe their message, they found words strong with all the strength of youth. When our Anglo-Saxon ancestors set out to translate those words, they too found words which everyone could understand; words which, alas! have now lost their meaning. It is time we made an endeavour to recover the old vitality. A crying need of the present age is to realise that other ages were alive, too; that the men of the first century were men of like passions with ourselves. When they hungered, they hungered as we do; when they suffered, they suffered as we do; when they quarrelled, as they sometimes did, they spoke out straight in their mother-tongue as we do. In a word, we have to think of them as men, and not as automata. But this we shall never do until the antique style in which a false reverence has made them speak is discarded for ever.

A version of the kind here indicated would not be easy to make. It would be hard, indeed, to steer between the Scylla of Wardour Street and the Charybdis of colloquialism: and it would require the collaboration of men of knowledge, taste, and skill. But it ought not to be impossible to collect such a body of men, and in time to produce a New

Testament worthy of the original and worthy of English as it now is. One thing we believe to be highly probable, that this translation, recalling but rarely the "familiar rhythms" of the Authorised Version, would rouse less irritation than those revisions which, retaining those rhythms as a general rule, are compelled to depart from them almost as soon as they are recalled, and inevitably therefore exasperate alike by their similarities and by their dissimilarities. That it will be an immense help to the translators themselves to be freed from a compulsory archaism, we are certain: the "Revised" translation of the Apocrypha, and specially of the Book of Wisdom, is an analogous case that fills us with hope. Nor is there any lack of attempts already made by competent hands—attempts which may serve as models or, occasionally, as warnings. We have already referred to one or two of these: Dr Rutherford's version of the Epistle to the Romans, Dr Weymouth's *New Testament in Modern Speech*, the *Twentieth Century New Testament*. To these might be added the rendering of Paul's Letters by Dr A. S. Way, that prince of translators, and of course Moffat's *Historical New Testament*. If our readers will compare the Authorised Version of I Cor. viii with that of the *Twentieth Century New Testament*, or the Revised Version of Rom. viii with that of Dr Rutherford or that of Dr Weymouth, they will see that in intelligibility at least there is no comparison. The Authorised Version is almost as obscure as if it were still Greek; the Revised not much better; while the modern translation at least has a meaning. As to fidelity in another sense—that of giving the reader some notion of the tone and force of the original—we appeal confidently to the candid and competent scholar to tell us whether the very worst of these modern versions is not a more accurate reflection of the true St Paul than either the Authorised Version of 1611 or the Revised of 1881.

V

MILTON AS MEDIEVALIST

THE obvious truth is often the enemy of a truth that is more obscure. When certain facts compel our attention, we sometimes neglect facts, equally important, which are a little less conspicuous. Our eyes, dazzled by the brightness, do not easily accommodate themselves to the shadow, and we stumble in consequence. Of this the common view of Milton is an exemplification. That he derived his inspiration primarily from the Scriptures and secondarily from the classical authors of Greece and Rome, is a truth that no one can miss, for it is forced upon our observation at every turn. *Paradise Lost*, in fact, is largely such a paraphrase of Genesis as Virgil might have made, had St Paul—as the Catholic hymn-writer wished—met him still alive in Rome. But it is equally true, and quite as important, that there is much that Virgil could not have written; that, in fact, Milton is simply saturated with medievalism, that he read the Scriptures in a medieval light, and that his study of the classics, while profound and wide, was touched at every turn by medieval influences. It has often, for instance, been observed—and we shall observe it ourselves later—how like certain passages of *Paradise Lost* are to the paraphrase of Caedmon. It has been noticed also by

Mr Verity, and, indeed, is obvious to everybody who can read Anglo-Saxon, that there are countless similarities between Milton's poems and the *Crist* of Cynewulf. In this latter case actual contact was impossible: it is certain that Milton never saw the *Crist*. Mr Verity explains the likeness by identity of inspiration—the Scripture. But this is surely not enough. No one, we maintain, could deduce the scheme of *Paradise Lost* from Scripture alone; such a deduction postulates a certain traditional mode of reading Scripture. And Cynewulf and Caedmon prove that this mode of reading, common to them with Milton, is not peculiar to him, but medieval.

In many respects, it is true, Milton is the morning star of modernity. But in many other respects he is the evening star of the Middle Ages; and justice cannot be done to him unless, while recognising his kinship with his peers, Isaiah, Homer, and Virgil, we also trace his descent from such men as the author of *Pearl*, or even from Hampole and Guillaume de Loris. Doubtless he scarcely recognised this ancestry himself; but possibly he dimly felt it when he confessed to Dryden that Spenser was his master. Not from Spenser, assuredly, did the most packed and pregnant of writers learn his style; but he may well have learned that mingling of Scripture with the classics, romance, and tradition which we find wild in Spenser and restrained in his disciple. And this mingling—this spirit which is willing to accept from all and sundry, the spirit of Boccaccio in the *Teseide* and of Ariosto in the *Orlando*—we mean here by medievalism. It is often undisciplined, it is often even riotous in its extravagance, but it is often alive; and it is this on its best side that gives most of the vitality to *Paradise Lost*, and, on its worst, crams the poem with those sermons and disquisitions which nearly prove its death.

Milton's debt to his predecessors may be illustrated in the minutest points as well as in the greatest. To take but an example or two from mere metre and prosody. Certain critics, from Addison downwards, have spent a long time in commenting on his peculiarities: on his habit of eliding or slurring the *y* at the end of words before a vowel, or an *o* in the same circumstances, or even a *u*. They have boggled at

> The excess
> Of glory' obscured,

or at

> To whom thus Eve, with perfect beauty' adorned,

or

> So were created, nor can'justly' accuse,

or at

> Damasco or Morocco' or Trebizond;

but they have not seldom failed to notice that these are not Miltonic innovations; they are *retentions* of old habits into a time when they were all but obsolete. Does Milton write "Virtue' in her shape how lovely," eliding or slurring the *ue*? What of

Chaucer's "The statue of Mars upon a cartë stood,"
or "The proudë King let make a statue of gold"?
Not one of these devices, indeed, but can easily be
paralleled from older writers. It is the purpose of
this paper to show how, in more important ways,
Milton reflects the opinions and cast of mind that
belonged to an earlier epoch.

And, first, note how the whole plan of *Paradise
Lost* involves the feudal conception of a revolt on
the part of some Robert de Belesme or Geoffrey de
Mandeville against his rightful lord. The rebellion
of Satan was treason, justly punished by forfeiture
of estates, by banishment, even by deprivation of
title. As the Duke of Aumerle rebelled against
Henry IV, so Satan rebelled against God. The former
suffered degradation in the peerage,

> Aumerle that was,
> But that is lost for being Richard's friend,
> And, madam, you must call him Rutland now.

So with the arch-rebel,

> Satan—so call him now; his former name
> Is heard no more in heaven.

Satan, like Bolingbroke, is exiled from his native
land, the only difference being that whereas to
Bolingbroke it is impossible "to hold a fire in his
hand by thinking on the frosty Caucasus," to Satan's
stronger nature

> The mind is its own place, and in itself
> Can make a heaven of hell, a hell of heaven.

So deeply ingrained is this idea in Milton's mind that we find him again and again using the technical feudal terms. Thus, for example, when Satan sees the punishment that has befallen the fellows or followers of his crime, we are greeted with the usual word for feudal deprivations, fines, or other penalties; he beholds

> Millions of spirits for his fault *amerced*
> Of heaven,

and we remember how in *Piers Plowman* the knights are bidden to let mercy be the taxer when they *amerce* their tenants. The words *imperial, sovereignty, thraldom*, occur at every turn. "He who now is sovran can dispose and bid," says Satan after the final conclusion of his war. "*Orders* and *degrees* jar not with liberty," he had said just before the war began. "Even in hell," says Beelzebub, "we have to do God *service* as His thralls by right of war." The *service* required in heaven was not hard in proportion to the good or benefice, confesses the repentant Satan.

It is no argument, all this, that Milton was himself a Republican, and that no one had been more distinguished than he for virulence of enmity against his King: nay, that many of the reasonings used by Satan against God are strikingly similar, both in matter and in word, to those used by Milton in *Eikonoklastes* or the *Defensio Populi* against Charles. Such inconsistencies are common enough in life, and one more need not greatly surprise us—though it *is* astonishing that Milton should have failed to see how damaging was the retort to which *Paradise Lost* laid itself open. But, as a matter of fact, to Milton it was Charles who was the real rebel, and Strafford his Beelzebub: nominally a monarch, Charles was essentially a usurper, and those who opposed him were supporters of the King *de jure*. Charles had rebelled against the Majesty of Law, and to him Milton would have spoken in language like that of Abdiel to Satan:

> Shalt thou give law to God? shalt thou dispute
> With Him the points of liberty, who made
> Thee what thou art, and formed the Powers of Heaven
> Such as He pleased, and circumscribed their being?

Charles had striven to break loose from constitutional restraints: and henceforth the laws he had broken would cease to be indulgent to him. But what we have here to notice is that, on whatever side Milton might be regarded as standing, whether for or against majesty, he viewed things in a medieval light and spoke of them in feudal terms. It was pride and, worse, ambition that threw Satan down, warring in heaven against heaven's matchless King. His puissance he thought to be his own, and he meant by proof to try who was his equal: he sent Abdiel as a kind of herald to renounce allegiance, refusing knee-tribute and prostration vile: he claimed the rights of prescription, and rejected with scorn the task of serving where "imperial title" had asserted that he was ordained to govern.

Now this view of Satan as a John Balliol solemnly defying an Edward I is not original in Milton, nor is it adopted simply from poetical convenience, or because the limitations of human nature compel a convention of the kind. It can be found everywhere in English literature from the earliest times down, at least, to the epoch of the Mystery Plays, with all their paraphernalia of challenges, trials, and tourneys. Whether Milton had actually read the so-called Caedmon is, as we have already hinted, doubtful; but his idea of Satan often agrees almost verbally with Caedmon's:

> The angel began to show pride;
> He raised himself against his high Liege-Lord,
> Hate-speech he used, defiance did he hurl,
> No thrall he chose to be of God, no vassal he;
> He deemed his might yet greater than his Lord's.

But then, says Caedmon, "the Mighty One was angry; he flung him down from his high seat; so had he lost favour with his overlord." The language of Milton is loftier than that of the Whitby herdsman; his meaning is precisely the same. And the conception is carried out into detail. Satan has his great nobles, each with his special power and duty. The "right" of holding the standard belongs to, and is claimed by, the tall cherub Azazel; the hellish hosts are ranged in regular order, from Thrones and

Dominations through Princedoms and Powers to the common herd: Satan, like Belshazzar, presides over a meeting of a thousand of his lords, while the churls and varlets throng without. And, when Satan wins his temporary victory, the various services done by his vassals are rewarded by appropriate benefices. Moloch and Chemosh, "the prime in order and in might," receive the highest posts and the richest demesnes, while lesser nobles obtain smaller and less honourable estates, until, in *Paradise Regained*, we find the conquered Air divided out much as England was parcelled by William the Norman among his followers.

In a poem such as *Paradise Lost* a certain amount of anthropomorphism is inevitable—if, indeed, it be not absolutely inevitable in all human attempts to reach the divine. And Milton confesses that, in order to accomplish his design at all, he has been driven to "liken spirits to corporeal forms." Yet we may be pardoned if we assume that the peculiar kind of anthropomorphism adopted in the poem is due to medieval influences. We know that to Milton it was not merely a poetic device, but one based on reality. In the second chapter of the *Treatise on Christian Doctrine* he declares his belief that God, "if not in fashion like unto man in all His parts and members, is of that form which He attributes to Himself in the sacred writings—at least as far as we are concerned to know": and in *Paradise Lost* itself, as every reader remembers, he asks the "leading question":

> What if earth
> Be but the shadow of heaven, and things therein
> Each to other like, more than on earth is thought?

In fact, Milton's pictorial imagination dominated him. He could not deal except in concrete images. His view of the Father was much the same as that of the Italian painters; his good angels, also, were those of a Giotto, or perhaps of a Michael Angelo; and if his Messiah differs, this was but because of his stern Arian Protestantism. Accepting from tradition the orders of angels, and adopting from painting such pictures as those of Uriel and Raphael, in which symbolism is lost in its representation, he drew his devils as angels, but tarnished. A medieval Satan, of course, he could not reproduce. To his sense of beauty and proportion such a Satan was intensely repugnant; and to his enormous pride it seemed impossible that an Adam (in whom he saw, more or less unconsciously, an image of himself) could ever have fallen before any foe less majestic than an Archangel ruined. A grotesque monster, with horns and tail, and all "the fee-faw-fum of Tasso and Klopstock," was not only beneath the dignity of poetry, but too contemptible to be regarded as a fitting enemy. Milton could conceive himself as yielding to a Strafford: the stage Mephistopheles he could only look on with scorn and disgust. And yet it is not hard to see that his Satan, though divested of many of his medieval trappings, remains medieval in his essence.

First, then, let us rid our minds of the almost purely modern notion of the "spiritual." All such phrases as a "principle of evil," a "something not ourselves that makes for righteousness," were outside of the medieval range of thought. To them, what are called "spiritual" beings were emphatically material—so material as, like the French knights at Poitiers, to be sadly encumbered by armour. By spirit is meant simply thin matter. The "substance" of Milton's angels is "airy," it is true; but there seems to be a certain proportion of earth and water in it. When Satan steers his flight aloft, incumbent on the dusky air of hell, it feels unusual weight; precisely as in *Inferno* the dilapidated crags move beneath the weight of Dante, or as the boat of Charon groaned under Aeneas. It may be hard, but it is not impossible, "to exclude this substance with corporeal bar"; the adamantine outside of the world excludes Satan, until he finds his way in through the opening that leads to heaven; and, though he despises the fence of Eden, yet he has at least to leap *over* it. All this is in the strictest medieval manner; for, as we have said, our ancestors were all but unable to conceive the non-corporeal. One curious parallel may here be cited. When Satan is wounded by Michael, he knows pain in the simplest human fashion; but we

are told that the airy substance soon united again.
In the Icelandic Saga of Thorstein Oxfoot, given in
Vigfusson's *Origines Islandicae* (ii. 585), we are told
how Thorstein went into a cairn where his ancestors
were buried, and how in consequence a feud arose
among the dead men. Thorstein could see "that
though the ghosts cut each other's hands and feet,
and dealt each other great wounds, they were healed
next moment, but the strokes that Thorstein dealt
them behaved naturally." Milton, then, conceived
of his angels as possessed of bodies similar to those
which Icelandic tradition gave to the dead; and those
bodies were solid enough. Indeed, Dunstan and
Luther themselves can scarcely have met a more
material devil than was Milton's Satan.

The very similes and metaphors by which Milton
endeavours to describe Satan are often medieval. It
has many times been noticed that the famous comparison with the Leviathan is from some *Physiologus*
or Middle Age natural history:

> Like that sea-beast
> Leviathan, whom God of all His works
> Created hugest, that swim the ocean-stream;
> Him haply slumbering on the Norway foam
> The pilot of some late night-foundered skiff
> Deeming some island, oft, as seamen tell,
> With fixed anchor in his scaly rind
> Moors by his side under the lee, while night
> Invests the sea, and wished morn delays.

This is nothing but the old medieval comparison *reversed* and ennobled. Of the dozen varieties of that story we may choose, as perhaps best, the Anglo-Saxon version in the Exeter Book, dating from before A.D. 1000. Doubtless Milton had seen the tale in some Latin setting:

> There is a whale called Fastitocalon, whose hue is like rough stone: whom seafarers deem, as they gaze on him, to be some island. Then moor they their high-stemmed ship to that *un-land*, and disembark thereon with courageous hearts: the keels stand fast by the staithe surrounded by the ocean-stream. On that island they kindle a fire; the men are glad of mind, rejoicing in their rest. Then feeleth the flame that strong one; and diveth straightway deep downward, seeking the bottom of the sea, and there in the death-chamber shutteth ship and crew together. *So is the wont of devils, and the fashion of fiends*, that they deceive men, and suddenly deal them doom when they expect not, hurling them down to hell.

Other Bestiaries call Fastitocalon "Aspedo," or some other name, but all agree in using him as a type of Satan. Milton compares Satan to *him*; but the comparison, as usual with him, is based on a certain identity: Satan is really physically huge, and lies prone on an actual lake. It is true that Milton does not, like Dante, take a tape measure into hell; but his conceptions are none the less concrete for being deliberately vague and inexact. And it is this "solidity and compound mass" in him which marks his relationship to Dante and sunders him from the ideal poets of later times. But the medievalism is not confined to forms of thought: it appears in matters of fact. The very plan for taking revenge on God by destroying His newly created world, and man as its denizen, which to so many people has seemed the hall-mark of Milton's genius, is as old as Teutonic Christianity, and might have sprung directly from an old Saga in which a vendetta is the central motive. A great chief injures you—you take vengeance by slaying one of his thralls; this is the story that turns up again and again in Icelandic and Germanic literature. Accordingly, the plant appears in full bloom in Caedmon:

He hath now marked out a world,
Where He hath wrought man after His likeness,
That He may henceforth repeople heaven
With bright souls. Therefore shall we gladly think thereon,
That we on Adam, if we ever can,
And on his children, may wreak our vengeance,
If so be we may contrive the way, to reward God with enmity,
For that He hath sundered us from the light of heaven.

The same idea, it is needless to say, occurs everywhere in literature throughout the Middle Ages. To name but one other passage, it is to be found in the famous poem of Eysteinn Asgrimsson, written about 1360, entitled *The Lily* [1].

---

[1] Satan presumes to match himself with God:

"aétlar sér við dýran dróttin
deila megn; enn hversu vegnar?"

Differences of detail there of course are. The usual medieval statement is that Lucifer, when beginning his revolt in heaven, drew after him the *tenth* part of heaven's host—*i.e.* one of the ten celestial orders, which are henceforth reduced to nine. According to Milton, the revolters included a *third* part of the heavenly army. Possibly, however, he had authority for his view, and a close search in the literature of the Middle Ages might find it. Again, according to the common story, Satan was three days in falling from heaven to hell: according to Milton, nine. Here also it is possible that he was not original. In the Scandinavian myth of Balder we are told that Hermod took *nine* days to go from Asgard to Hel: "that is to say of Hermod, that he rode nine nights through

he falls headlong like a plummet with his companions:

> "søktist hann með sínum grønnum
> sem blývarða í djúpleik jarðar."

God then makes the world—"starting a new fashion"—and sets man therein: but to test his merit gives him *one* command. Then Satan swells with rage, curses the ban under which he lives, and grudges that the tribes of men should have on earth the bliss that he has forfeited; therefore "brewing the dregs of death he, knowing magic arts, disguises himself from the eyes of men, and in the form of a serpent utters forth his voice":

> "þrútnar, svellr, ok unir við illa
> engill bann þat er hafþi fengit,
> fyrðasveitin faedd á jørðu
> fái þar vist, er sjálfr hann misti;
> ok bruggandi dauðans dreggjar
> duldist hann fyr augsjón manna
> fjǫlkunnigr; í einum innan
> ormi tók hann mál at forma."

All this might be an "argument" of *Paradise Lost.*

dark vales and deep, so that he saw not until he came to the river Gjoll, and rode over Gjoll-bridge." Not improbably, in the blending of Christianity with heathen myth, these nine days were retained in some legend known to Milton in a Latin dress.

If, however, there be one point more than another on which all medieval mythologists are agreed, it is that Satan, in starting his rebellion, drew his army to the north. The origin of this idea can scarcely be doubted. To our ancestors the north was the region of cold, of mists, of horror, of the Thurses and monsters, such as Hrungnir or Thrym, who personified the dread unknown. Jotunheim, the abode of the Jotuns or giants, was to the north of Asgard, the home of the gods. To propitiate these beings, men naturally turned to the north, and hence the Christians, who bent toward the east, came to use *horfa i northr*, to look northward, as a phrase for heathen worship. Grimm, in his *Deutsche Mythologie*, gives a score of examples of this belief. "Diabolus sedet in lateribus aquilonis," says Gregory. When a heathen charm was sung, the singer *leit i northr*, looked to the north. "Down toward the north lies Hel-way," says the Icelandic Edda. Waterfalls that run northward are the abodes of demons. "Lucifer," declares Rabanus Maurus, "traxit ad inferni sulfurea stagna, in gelida aquilonis parte ponens sibi tribunal." Lucifer "chot sizzin nordin" is the phrase of a High-German writer;

nay, to wish a man at the north was a medieval way of wishing that the devil might get him.

Of this belief Milton makes full use in *Paradise Lost*[1]. Thus speaks the Father to the Son (v. 724 *seq.*):

> Such a foe
> Is rising, who intends to erect his throne
> Equal to Ours throughout the spacious north;

and later we learn that Satan has already advanced

> Unto the limits of the north.

But the great chief is not the only one of the devils who is medieval in origin. All his followers, with possibly two exceptions, belong to the same family. The story given in *Paradise Lost* of their fall, of their subsequent eruption from hell, and of their dominion over air and over regions of the earth, nay, their very names, are part and parcel of the mythology current in the Middle Ages. That mythology, it is now known, was very early elaborated into something like consistency; it occurs in the Book of Enoch; but the form in which it came to Milton was traditional. As Sir Walter Raleigh points out, it is found fully set out in Hooker's *Ecclesiastical Polity*:

Being dispersed, some in the air, some in the earth, some in the water, some among the minerals, dens, and caves that are under the earth, they have by all means laboured to effect

---

[1] Of course it would please him to remember that he had here the added authority of Holy Writ. Lucifer sat "on the mount of congregation in the uttermost parts of the north" (Isaiah xiv. 13: cp. *Paradise Lost*, v. 755, 766).

a universal rebellion against the laws, and as far as in them lieth utter destruction of the works of God. These wicked spirits the heathen honoured instead of gods, both generally under the name of *dii inferi*, gods infernal, and particularly, some as household gods, some as nymphs; in a word, no foul or wicked spirit which was not one way or other honoured of men as god, till such time as light appeared in the world, and destroyed the works of the Devil.

The belief, then, that Moloch, Chemosh, Jove, and Saturn were in reality devils masquerading as gods, was not held by Milton merely as a poetic convention, but as literally true; for he was the last man to draw a wide distinction between poetry and veracity: and this belief was in his time practically universal. To our own English ancestors, for example, Thor and Odin, nay Mohammed himself, were literal devils; Thor's hammer was a clever mimicry of the Cross, and the Crescent a magical symbol scarcely inferior in efficacy to the Christian scutcheon. Milton's devils were not, it is true, contemptible beings; yet we may be sure that it was not Milton the classicist, but Milton the medievalist, who made a devil of Apollo. Similarly, it is not Milton the lover of secular learning who ascribes to demons a love of philosophic argumentation, but Milton the successor of Thomas Aquinas and of the divines who imprisoned Roger Bacon[1]. There is the

[1] The devil who dragged Montefeltro down to hell from the very hands of St Francis did it by *argument*: "Forse tu non pensavi ch' io loico fossi": "You forgot, apparently, that I was a logician!" (*Inferno,* XXVII. 122).

same contradiction between the admirer of Galileo and the poet who represents God as laughing at the quaint opinions of astronomers. In Milton, it must never be forgotten, the classical and the Teutonic were always struggling; sometimes the one prevailed and sometimes the other, but neither was ever wholly suppressed. It is not necessary to believe with Monsignor Barnes that he was a Catholic at heart and died in that faith, in order to realise his indebtedness to the old religion. His grandfather was a Catholic and his brother became one; and fragments of emotional sympathy still lived in the determined intellectual opponent of the Papacy. It is this sympathy which explains the presence in *Paradise Lost* of an Anselmian theory of the Atonement. It is this sympathy which accounts for the strange intermingling of allegory with the historicity of the poem; an allegorising tendency which is scarcely inferior to that of Gregory the Great or of Guillaume de Loris, and which stirred Addison to utter astonishment.

Similarly medieval in spirit is the cosmography, if so it can be called, on which the system of *Paradise Lost* is based. The map of Infinitude, as drawn by Masson, shows us what was Milton's conception. Half of the All is occupied by heaven, which is defended by crystal battlements like the walls of Asgard as seen by King Gylfi, and the underpart of which is crystal also—indeed, sufficiently transparent for the light of heaven to penetrate some distance into Chaos. In fact, heaven is like the "crystal clyffe ful relusaunt" from which "many a royal ray did rere," as seen by the imagination of the poet of *Pearl* in the fourteenth century. From the exact centre of this hangs the World, our Universe, pendent by golden chains (like the chain of Ambition in Spenser), adamantine on the outside, and only to be entered, even by celestial spirits, through an opening at the top. At the centre of the World is our Earth—for Milton, as philosopher, seems to have been Copernican, but as poet was Ptolemaic. At the traditional place in Earth, of course, he puts Eden; and the garden of Paradise, in full accord with the same tradition, is set on a hill in Eden: the rose, as the early Church taught, is without thorn there, and the season was a perpetual spring until, after Adam's fall, the axis of the earth was pushed out of the perpendicular:

> Some say, He bid His angels turn askance
> The poles of earth twice ten degrees and more
> From the sun's axle; they with labour pushed
> Oblique the centric globe...else had the spring
> Perpetual smiled on earth with verdant flowers,
> Equal in days and nights.

Hence the seasons' difference, that "penalty of Adam" of which the Duke in *As You Like It* complains. The whole description of Paradise, indeed, whether of the celestial or of the terrestrial variety, is traditional to almost the last detail. Those who doubt this statement may read *Barlaam and Josaphat*, or even the few lines quoted from it in Verity (Milton, *Paradise Lost*, III. iv. 109).

Beneath the World, at exactly the distance of the World's radius from it, lies Hell-gate, guarded like the castle in the *Romance of the Rose* by a portress, and connected with the World by a bridge, built after the Fall by Sin and Death, which reminds us, as it has reminded many others, of the ladder in the Faust-book by which the demons ascend to their abode. Hell-bound is apparently conceived of as a spherical surface, convex to heaven; and this abode, again in full agreement with the medieval doctrine, was prepared for the rebel angels just before their fall. "Before the fall of my Lord Lucifer was no hell, but even then was hell ordained," says the Faust-book.

Apart from these three regions, Heaven, the World, and Hell, all the rest is Chaos, a turbulent and uncontrollable ocean, in which perpetual night reigns, and Chance, "high arbiter," governs all, while hot, cold, moist, and dry, four fierce champions, strive eternally for mastery, as, according to medieval physicians, they strive in the bodies of human beings. Out of this weltering mass God has cut the World with golden compasses; and apparently Hell has been marked off in like manner. Hell itself, though it has a lake of liquid fire and land ever burning with solid flame, has its regions of polar cold, to which the damned are brought at certain seasons that they may experience the extremes of punishment made more fierce by change—a variety of the hideous Caina and Giudecca of Dante, themselves developments of older notions. But all along we are in the grip of the Middle Ages, whose untamed imagination revelled in the invention of horrors, some of which were but too closely mimicked in castle and dungeon. Little wonder that our ancestors dreaded death even more than we do. We think of the natural terrors of poor Claudio, who so shudderingly feared

> To bathe in fiery floods, or to reside
> In thrilling region of thick-ribbed ice;
> To be imprisoned in the viewless winds,
> And blown with restless violence round about
> The pendent world.

Milton is not usually grotesque; but this mapping-out of infinitude and this picturing of the unknown, enormously powerful and terrific as it is, is as grotesque as anything in Dante or even in St Patrick's Purgatory. And the reason is obvious: like the cosmography of Dante, this cosmography is "medieval"; that is, it is a strange mixture of Teutonic mythology and Ptolemaic astronomy, overlaid with conceptions borrowed from the various Apocalypses, of which that of St John is only one. Allied to all this is the mere dwelling on horrors apparently for their own sake, as in the descriptions of death and hell so often indulged in by monkish preachers. The Lazar-house passage in the eleventh Book, with the forty or fifty lines that follow, might be a chapter from Innocent III's *De Miseria Conditionis Humanae*, a work, as is well known, immensely popular in the Middle Ages, and one which exercised a strange fascination over so cheerful a mind as Chaucer's. That the suggestion for these passages seems often to have come from such writers as Seneca and Juvenal is but an added argument; for it was precisely these writers that, of all the classics, appealed most forcibly to the Middle Ages.

And finally, is it too fanciful to imagine that it was the working of Early England within him, rather than the example of Latin, Greek, or Italian, that led Milton to the use of blank verse for his epic? The "ancient liberty *recovered* to heroic poem from the troublesome and modern bondage of riming," of which he speaks in his famous preface on *The Verse*, may well have been the liberty of Caedmon and Cynewulf. He may have heard from Junius that Caedmon and his contemporaries did not rhyme, and this knowledge may have aided, more or less unconsciously, his impulse to freedom. In this connection we may be allowed to quote from Sir Israel Gollancz's introduction to his edition of the *Crist*:

What better instrument for the grand epic style than the wondrous blank verse of these ancient poets? Critics delight to dwell on the "mighty line" created by the greatest of Shakespeare's predecessors; but, ten centuries before Marlowe's genius impressed itself on the English drama, English poetry had already "unlocked the secret of blank verse, and had played upon its hundred stops." The secret of Marlowe's great discovery lies in this, that he Teutonised the *versi sciolti* imported from Italy, and unconsciously imparted thereto the flexibility and vigour that characterised the national metre used by the oldest of English poets.

The greatest of Marlowe's pupils, greater even than his master, and assuredly not less "Teutonic" than he, was the Milton of *Paradise Lost.*

vi

I WELL remember how, in early days, after reading Macaulay's essay on Milton, who was then the god of my idolatry, I was seized with the desire to verify for myself, like a second Robert Hall, the correctness of the parallel there drawn between *Paradise Lost* and the *Divine Comedy*. Nor could I rest until I had procured a copy of Longfellow's translation, and, with all the zeal of fifteen years, had started on my self-imposed task. Although, of course, there was much that I did not understand, my interest was very great, and I did not stop until I had finished the whole poem, from the Dark Forest to the Love that moves the sun and the other stars. What boy, indeed, that had any fondness for poetry, could fail to be moved by the pride of Farinata, by the glorious last adventure of Ulysses, or by the stories of Francis and of Dominic? I still possess that copy of Longfellow, and the marks show with what care I perused every line, every note, and every "illustration." But I remember a strange and ever-increasing sense of bewilderment. Where was the likeness to Milton? The further I went, the greater seemed the dissimilarity; until at last I felt I could as soon have compared the *Excursion* to the *Lady of the Lake* as the *Divine Comedy* to *Paradise Lost*.

For some time, indeed, I was inclined to ascribe this bewilderment to the extraordinary prosiness of Longfellow's version, which is, after all, little better than a metrical "crib." Dante, I had been led to expect, might differ from Milton in his style of description, and in the use to which he puts his similes and metaphors; but he was yet, I had supposed, essentially of the same kind. Such parts of Cary's translation as I had seen only confirmed this impression; for Cary, whatever style he had actually achieved, had obviously aimed at being Miltonic. I fancied therefore that, if but Longfellow had been able to render Dante in a worthy fashion, the likeness between the two great poets, at present so completely disguised, might have been revealed. And yet, I could hardly imagine that in the mere process of being turned with absolute literality from one language into another, a poem could entirely lose its character and assume the opposite.

The years went by, until I was able to take up Dante again—this time in the original; and now came the answer to my problem. Longfellow was not altogether responsible for the trouble. Dante and Milton, *as poets*, ought never to be compared; they have perhaps nothing in common beyond that quality which all poets of the first magnitude must inevitably show. As men, it is true, they reveal many likenesses: they have the same indomitable aristocratic pride; both were lonely and haughty exiles in a land that knew them not; both had the hate of hate and the scorn of scorn; both alike knew themselves to be above the ordinary human stature; both alike were deficient in humour, finding a substitute for it in a furious contempt or a kind of grotesque and boisterous jocularity: had they met as men, they might have greeted each other as peers. But as poets they may or may not be peers—they are at any rate as far asunder as the poles: and Macaulay, in coupling the two, had misled me as I believe he has misled others. The difference is plain and total. Whereas Dante is a mystic and deals in symbol, Milton is one of the most concrete and direct of great poets. And this difference works itself out in a curious and paradoxical way—an effect on which Macaulay, as is his manner, dwells more at length than on its cause. Milton, treating his subject thus concretely, and as it were historically, finds it less, and not more, necessary than Dante to describe his scenes with precision and particularity. His visions, to mix our metaphors, are open and above-board; he can describe them therefore by allusion or by more or less distant parallel. Dante, on the contrary, to whom the thing symbolised is all in all, is constrained by the very nature of his purpose to describe the *symbol* precisely and clearly, in order that his readers may form (within the limits prescribed by the character of the theme) clear ideas of the thing symbolised. Thus the very mysticism of Dante leads him to a certain almost prosy definition, whereas the unmystical Milton often shows a Shelleyan vagueness. Somewhat as the voyages of Gulliver have to be mapped out with all the lines of the Indies, *because* the real voyages were taken by Dean Swift in European drawing-rooms, so the travels of Dante have to be mapped out because the real travels were made within his own heart. Milton may, so to speak, content himself with a mere reference to a known geography; Dante must himself draw his charts. But this precision marks him as not less, but more, of a mystic. He dwells in abstractions; and the rocks he climbs or the rivers he passes are really as unsubstantial as those that saw the feet of Alastor.

Both, of course, were didactic poets—in this sense, that they would have refused to speak without a message, and that "art for art's sake" would have been to them a phrase without a meaning. And to both the message clothed itself in theological forms: they desired to teach men the nature of God, the significance of sin which alienates men from God, and the means of reconciliation. But whereas Milton views God, in his pictorial fashion, as a Person, Dante, despite his Catholic creed, views Him as a principle. The duty of man, according to the one, is to know and understand Him; the duty of man, according to the other, is to grow into Him; nor was ever a St Teresa or a John of the Cross more absorbed into God than is Dante at the end of his infinite journey. To speak with perhaps a touch of exaggeration, Milton wishes to greet the Supreme Ruler as a subject, but a subject safe-guarded by constitutions and charters; Dante longs to break down his own personality and to open the gates of his being to the inrush of the divine. To Dante the will of God *is* our peace; it is scarcely over-emphasising the case to say that to Milton man and God sign a *treaty* of peace: that the One commands and the other obeys is merely an incident. Between the two views there lies all the space that separates a Calvin from a Tauler.

Both poets, again, it goes without saying, recognise sin as an abuse of free will; and both are faced with the difficulty of reconciling the omnipotence of a good God with His omniscience; but Dante (to whom, as to St Thomas Aquinas, even hell is a manifestation of the love of God) sees sin as an alien body intruded into the great unity, to be absorbed and reconciled by an all-embracing Love: whereas to Milton it is a rebellion, to be crushed by superior power; and, though the Power is informed with love, it is not love itself. Both believe that the enlightened mind will in time see the goodness lurking behind the apparent cruelty of things; but Dante believes that this will come when the Many are rapt into the One; Milton, when the Many, though still proudly retentive of their isolation, realise their dependence on the Sovereign. Thus, to take a single consequence of this general diversity, to Dante the doctrine of a Triune God presented no difficulty; for the Manifold after all is but the phantasmal: to Milton the absolute impenetrability of each individual ego was a first axiom. So soon as God has created a person, whether that person be an Adam or a Messiah, the person stands apart, alone, and autonomous. Hence not only was Milton an Arian in his overtly theological works, but *Paradise Lost* is an Arian poem.

This, then, is one difference, and a vast one, between Milton and Dante. There are scores of others, of which time would fail us to mention more than one or two. Their *styles*, for instance, so far as we can isolate style from personality, are altogether unlike. Dante is constantly varying; like Homer, he "rises and falls with his subject"; Milton, allowance being made for the lapses inevitable to humanity, is ever the same. Dante *can* be sublime—not even the early books of *Paradise Lost* are more sublime than some parts of the *Paradiso*—but he would seem to prefer the plain and unadorned, and to gain his effects, like Demosthenes, by brevity, reticence, and the emphasis of the bare phrase. Both alike love to pack the utmost meaning into a sentence; but Dante stops because he has said enough; Milton because he has said something allusive which is meant to make his reader complete the picture for himself. The style of the *Inferno* is, as a rule, no more adorned than that of Caesar's *Commentaries*, and for the same reason; he wants us to believe that he "has been there." Milton's Hell is terrible, but it is magnificent: it enchants because it is distant.

Having seen this impassable gulf that separates the two great poets, I was led to consider whether Milton himself might not have felt it; and a casual remark of a friend urged me further: "Do you really think that Milton cared much for Dante?" I reflected again that it is not very often one lights on a critic who really cares equally for both. It is certain that such a critic must be a man of peculiarly catholic and unprejudiced mind. Landor, for example, the admirer and imitator of Milton, is assuredly hardly just to Dante; and all readers of Ruskin must have noticed how, whenever he has occasion to quote a passage from the *Divine Comedy*, he insists on dragging in a disparaging judgment, often gratuitously challenging, on Milton. That, in most of the passages he quotes, Milton was making not the slightest effort to do what Dante was doing; that, in fact, the end he aimed at was of quite another kind, does not prevent Ruskin from depreciating him in season and out of it. I was led, then, to consider whether Milton himself, though of course admiring his great predecessor, did not admire him with reservations, and whether his admiration, like that of Landor, was not mingled with a good deal of repulsion.

Proof of this suspicion, if at all possible, must be indirect: for the overt references to Dante in Milton's works are singularly few. There is first the famous allusion in the *Sonnet to Lawes*:

> Dante shall give Fame leave to set thee higher
> Than his Casella, whom he wooed to sing,
> Met in the milder shades of Purgatory;

from which it is obviously plain that nothing definite can be gathered, unless indeed one may hazard the guess that Milton, like most of the admirers of Dante who are not devotees, preferred the *Purgatorio* to the other two parts of the *Comedy*.

There is also the quotation in the *Treatise of Reformation in England* from the nineteenth canto of *Inferno*:

> Ah, Constantine, of how much ill was cause,
> Not thy conversion, but those rich domains
> That the first wealthy Pope received of thee;

followed by an allusion to *Paradiso*, xx. 55:

> L' altro che segue, con le leggi e meco,
> Sotto buona intenzion che fe' mal frutto,
> Per cedere al pastor, si fece Greco.
> Ora conosce come il mal dedutto
> Dal suo bene operar, non gli è nocivo,
> Avvegna che sia il mondo indi distrutto.

But in both these passages he is quoting not so much Dante the poet as the Dante whom he would fain claim as half a Protestant: and it is noteworthy that a few lines further down he speaks of Petrarch and Ariosto as, though later in date than Dante, his equals in fame (*Prose Works*, ed. Bohn, ii. 383); thus, it may be, giving us to understand that he was not conscious of the immense distance that divides these poets, great as they are in their way, from their mighty predecessor. In other places, again, he speaks of Tasso as if he put him on the highest peak of Italian poetry. It is hardly possible for one who thus regards Tasso to feel an unstinted admiration for Dante.

It is remarkable, further, how few, despite the similarity of subject, are the imitations of the *Comedy* in *Paradise Lost*; indeed the clearest imitation in all Milton's works seems to me to be not in the epic but in the *Arcades*, where one would think the "smooth enamelled green"—a phrase, by the way, for which Milton has been ignorantly censured—is derived from the "verde smalto" of *Inferno*, iv. 118, as the parallel phrase in *Comus*, "the azure sheen of turquoise blue and emerald green" has also a Dantesque air. In the Miltonic hell there are "regions of sorrow, *doleful* shades, where hope never comes," reminding us, perhaps rightly, of the "città dolente," into which those who enter must abandon all hope; and there are some other resemblances, perhaps accidental, between the hells of the two poets. Both alike picture extremes of fire and ice, extremes made by change more fierce, in the infernal realms. When Satan, rising on the air, compels it to feel an unusual weight, one could believe that Milton, though mainly following Virgil, has an eye on the boat of Phlegyas; and there are points in the description of Lethe which equally seem to show a double dependence, on the Roman and on the Florentine. Nor is it easy to believe that the description, in Book XI of *Paradise Lost*, of the lazar-house, with its "demoniac frenzy, moping melancholy, and moonstruck madness," was written without some thought of the sighs, plaints, and groans of the half-damned cowardly refusers in the outer court of Inferno. But, when all possible allusions, distinct or faint, have been collected, I think the reader will be surprised they are not more numerous[1].

Nor is there any sign, throughout Milton's works, that he ever considered himself as a rival of Dante: or even that he felt for him the admiration (tempered, it is true) which was felt by Chaucer, and repeatedly

---

[1] There are, it is true, commentators who see an imitation of another passage of Dante in the lines above referred to (*Paradise Lost*, XI. 494):

"Sight *so deform* what heart of rock could long
Dry-eyed behold? Adam could not, but wept,
Though not of woman born; compassion quelled
His best of man, and gave him up to tears";

comparing the pity of Dante at the sight of the distorted astrologers (*Inferno*, XX. 20):

"Com' io potea tener lo viso asciutto
Quando la nostra imagine da presso
Vidi sì *torta?*"

and they see in the rebuke of Virgil the source of Michael's speech to Adam. But the likeness is slight, and were it much closer might well and ungrudgingly expressed; and this though Chaucer is, if possible, more direct and concrete than Milton himself. Those with whom Milton challenged comparison—"blind Thamyris and blind Maeonides"— were quite of a different class from Dante; and, though he chose religion for his theme, he treated it as they (and not as Dante) dealt with their themes. To him religion was a matter mainly of testimony; and the argument of *Paradise Lost* presented itself as but an historical subject, higher than that of Arthur or Aeneas, but of essentially the same order. It was literally true; and its symbolic meaning was only secondary; whereas to Dante, as to all his kin from Philo and Origen downwards, the literal was comparatively unimportant, and the allegorical all but everything. Thus, to take an example which we may

be fortuitous; for it is difficult to believe that Milton had not here in mind the Shakespearean words (*Henry V*, iv. vi. 30):

> "But I had not so much of man in me,
> And all my mother came into mine eyes
> And gave me up to tears."

The lines in *Samson Agonistes*,

> "The sun to me is dark
> And silent as the moon,"

have been thought to be a reminiscence of Dante (*Inferno*, i. 60),

> "Mi ripingeva là dove il sol tace";

and the reader will remember that the mention of this parallel led to the friendship between Gray and Norton Nicholls. But here again I believe that, if borrowed at all, the phrase was taken directly from the classics, as the word "interlunar" in the next line suggests. We know that the times when the moon is invisible were called in Rome either "silentia" or "interlunia."

have occasion to use again, to Milton the Almighty is an infinite human being, invisible because of the light that surrounds His throne. His skirts are dark with excess of bright; but to Dante the Almighty *is* light, and is never mentioned throughout the whole poem except by periphrasis or symbol.

This is the explanation of the fact we pointed out at the beginning. It is a great mistake to imagine that there is no definition in Milton's cosmography; but it is not on this that he desires to dwell; he is like an historian who takes the use of a map by his readers more or less for granted. Conversely, while to Dante the details are in themselves uninteresting, what they symbolise is so full of meaning that he marks them with Defoe-like exactness—an exactness sometimes, to our ideas, bordering on the grotesque. Similarly, with notes of time: these are not absent in Milton, but he can rely on the reader to know the rough outline of his story, and need not therefore insist on them: whereas Dante, whose story is new, must put down almost every minute of his itinerary. To him the interest lay in an inner story, a "Grace Abounding to the Chief of Sinners"; Milton was not without this interest, but his aim in his poem was to tell a history of the external past.

It might almost seem as if Milton often went deliberately out of his way to avoid contact with Dante; as, to compare great things with lesser, Swinburne or Morris went out of his way to avoid contact with Tennyson. We know quite well when Milton is touching the shield of Homer, or when he robs Virgil of an episode or a phrase; but Dante, of whom he must have thought at every turn, he for the most part passes by. For him, the mystic poet, despite his outward definiteness, was too vaporous and unsubstantial; to have contended with *him* would have been to wrestle with the air. Thus his Italian sonnets, I believe, echo the *Laura* rather than the *Vita Nuova*—with which, indeed, so far as I know, Milton shows no acquaintance. From Ariosto, again, with whom, despite a vein of light fantasy and fiction, he doubtless recognised some kinship, he scrupled not to borrow a whole canto for his sixth book: by a sort of reversed parody he transforms the Ferrarese fire-arms into the artillery of heaven: but from the Florentine there is no theft of nearly the same magnitude. Milton felt himself to be a narrative poet; and it was to the great narrators that he went for his models; not to the weavers of allegories.

Once again, however, it is necessary to qualify. Though so concrete a poet, Milton knew well that more must be meant in poetry than meets the ear; and he knew that in a sense all poetry must be allegorical, nor least such poetry as his own and Spenser's, which was intended to teach. He would have agreed with Protagoras as against Socrates that the bards are the true instructors; and he would have said that if they write history, their history is a philosophy none the less. To him, then, Satan is not a mere Strafford; he is also Rebellion: and if the fallen angels are revolted vassals, sin itself, as he tells us in his Divorce pamphlet, is an alien and revolted vassal also, which has cast off the free citizenship of heaven. Eve is not solely a woman, she is woman incarnate; in the loins of Adam are all his sons—nay, the primal form of humanity itself. We do not need the *Prose Works* to tell us that the Universe is not extension only but thought as well. Heaven, though its distance from earth is calculated, is none the less within us: and hell, though measured, is not a place only, but a state of mind. Milton was in harmony with those philosophers of whom he speaks in the *Discipline of Divorce*, who thought it "not a punishment so proper and proportionate for God to inflict, to banish for ever into a local hell, deeper from holy bliss than the world's diameter multiplied, as to punish sin with sin." Cicero was right in believing that God has no severer penalty for man than to make him more sinful. It is but a natural corollary of this that parts of *Paradise Lost* are almost ostentatiously allegorical; and it was for want of seeing this that the older critics, like Addison, found fault with Milton for introducing them into the midst of what they regarded as but history splendidly versified. Such are the episode of Sin and Death, the Paradise of Fools, and the incident of the trans-

formation of Satan and his angels into hissing ser-
pents: while lesser instances might be collected from
every part of the poem. But here again how different
from Dante's method! These are, so to speak, literal
allegory, told in direct narrative; Dante is symbol:
these admit of an easy and swift explanation; Dante
eludes analysis, and when we think we have found
one solution we are led on to another.

But the chief distinction—or rather the chief way
in which the distinction between the two poets
exhibits itself—is this. Milton was a man, and he
put into mankind much of his own masculine pride
and dignity. Regarding Adam as but John Milton
in other circumstances and another age, he refused
to allow him to fall before an ignoble enemy. Thus,
though he admired Tasso, he would not have a
Tassonian devil; and, had he known Goethe, he
would have equally rejected the scoffing Mephistopheles. Satan, before whom the noble and goodly
Adam is to give way, must himself be great and
noble, dealing in temptations like those he put before
the Son of God in the wilderness; having something
great to offer—dominion, knowledge, the resistless
oratory that shook the Arsenal and fulmined over
Greece. He must resemble the Hannibal before
whom the Romans were not ashamed of yielding at
Cannae; he storms Chaos as the Carthaginian stormed
the Alps; a magnified man—Milton could conceive
nothing higher—with vices on a great scale, but

balanced by great virtues; who goes first into the battle, and retires last from it; who is undefeated by extremes of heat and cold; whose body cannot be broken by fatigue, and whose mind is never crushed by disaster. We may be sure that Milton was repelled by Dante's demons, and was full of scorn that such creatures should win victories over men made in the image of God. *His* hell should know no Malacoda or Alichino; his Satan should be no Lucifer; his Beelzebub should be a statesman or diplomatist of a Wolsey's calibre; his Moloch a warrior of the Mezentius kind; even his Belial should show at least external grace and beauty. For him, even damnation has its dignity; and many of Dante's punishments must have seemed to him unbeseeming the God that deals them. That they are adapted to the sin would not have redeemed them in his eyes; for the sins which appealed to him, and which alone he could fancy himself committing, were all of the lofty kind. Of all Dante's damned, indeed, unless we can make an exception in favour of Diomede and Ulysses, I imagine that Farinata alone would have commanded Milton's respect. Inferno itself, with its grotesqueries, its despicable denizens, its vulgar blasphemies, he despised, and substituted for it a Pandemonium that outshone the glories of Babylon and Great Alcairo: for to Milton hell itself, like earth, must be at least a shadow of heaven, or it is unworthy to enter into conflict with it. God, unlike Gibbon,

must not be humiliated by a victory over contemptible antagonists.

Hence, perhaps, the one conspicuous point in
which Milton is inferior to Dante—his representation of the Supreme. For the very same reason that
his demons stand so much higher, his Deity is in-
definitely lower. He had not sufficiently pondered
the lesson which Paul learnt from his vision—that
it is not lawful for men to utter the things seen and
heard in that region. For a representation of the
Divine, hint and symbol are alone possible: Milton's
direct method fails here, and Dante's, so far as
humanity can succeed, succeeds. Milton, like Dante,
knew that God is light; but he was hampered by his
theological view that "as far as we are concerned
to know, He is of that form which he attributes to
himself in the sacred writings"; that "we ought to
entertain such a conception of him, as he, in con-
descending to our capacities, has shown that he
desires we should conceive" (*Prose Works*, IV. 17).
God has, so far as we have a right to inquire, passions, parts, dimensions; he repents, is weary, rests
from toil, walks in a garden in the cool of the day.
Not of course that God in his essence is thus human;
but that it does not befit men to use any other image
to represent him than such as He himself has chosen
as the most appropriate for our faculties. If we think
then that the picture of the Father given us in *Paradise Lost* is a low one, Milton replies, "Let us require

no better authority than God himself for determining what is worthy or unworthy of him"; for "he would never say or direct anything to be written of himself, which is inconsistent with the opinion he wishes us to entertain of his character." Thus the blame must be cast on the Scriptures, and not on Milton himself. Nevertheless, the blame is just; and the advance of a true understanding of Scripture has, in this respect, weakened the hold of Milton on the world. Much as a similar advance has diminished the power over us of Dante's descriptions of hell, so has the power of Milton's descriptions of heaven been weakened; whereas, in the choice of images to convey an idea of Paradise, Dante has been better advised. But our point here is not the absolute merit of Dante, but what Milton is likely to have thought of him; and here again we are not left without light. The *Treatise of Christian Doctrine* supplies us with our answer. He would have charged Dante, as he charges others, with "anthropopathy"; that is, with a neglect of the Scriptures and with an undue indulgence of his own fancies. We might imagine that it is to Dante himself he is alluding, when he says, "It is on this very account that God has lowered himself to our level, lest in our flights above the reach of human understanding, and beyond the Written Word, we should be tempted to indulge in vague cogitations and subtleties." Strangely enough, therefore, it is because of one of Milton's few lapses into awed humility, that he has laid himself open to the charge of undue presumption. Through his very fear of seeming to know too much about God, he has been accused of too great familiarity with Him.

But be this as it may, it would appear that our suspicion is justified, and that Milton, while admiring, as everyone must admire, the immense power of the Florentine poet, was repelled by many of his qualities, and that, while traversing so much of the same ground, he was careful not to tread in his steps. And, when we consider these mighty geniuses together, we shall perforce call them "magis pares quam similes."

Note. I ought to have mentioned that Professor Garrod (*Essays and Studies of the English Association*, Vol. XII, 1926, p. 17) seems inclined to trace 'enamelled green' to Chapman's *Shadow of Night*: but this does not preclude an earlier origin.

vii

"NEXT to Shakespeare," says Coleridge, "I am not certain whether Thomas Fuller, beyond all other writers, does not excite in me the sense and emotion of the marvellous." It was the reading of the *Church History of Britain* that drew this encomium from Coleridge; and we believe that, due allowance being made for some natural exaggeration, most readers of that history will concur in the judgment. The wit, practical wisdom, common sense, love of truth, breadth of mind, shown in the book are indeed astonishing; and that they all blend into a harmonious whole is more remarkable still. Fuller's interests were all in serious things; he wrote sermons, biographies of great men, chronicles of the Crusades, devotional tracts; yet his touch is as light as that of Addison, and his sallies as keen as those of Bernard Shaw. Almost every page contains two or three pointed sayings; and yet, unlike Seneca, La Rochefoucauld, and other sententious writers, he did not *seek* for point; it came unbidden, and was the natural overflow of a quaint and richly endowed mind. He discourses on Church councils, and makes them as interesting as football matches. Not Macaulay himself is more indifferent to what is called the "dignity of history"; but he is as zealous for truth as Thucydides or Hallam. Withal he was a man of peculiarly lovable, kindly, and generous temper; and in his works the man is ever visible behind the author. Hence it is doubtful whether there are, in the whole range of English literature, books more uniformly delightful than his. As he himself, with a pardonable pride, remarks, not one of them failed of popularity in his lifetime; and the lapse of three centuries has lent them that flavour of the antique which makes them even more attractive to us than they were to his contemporaries.

His style, which won rapturous praise, and the more subtle compliment of imitation, from Charles Lamb, is a product of that happy age in which the divorce between written prose and daily talk had not yet been made absolute: it is full of the raciness of conversation, and does not hesitate at times to avail itself of the resources of slang. He can, like Milton, use a Latin vocabulary; but, like Milton, he loves to clinch a sentence with a good vigorous Anglo-Saxon word, while, unlike him, he does not form his sentences on the classical periodic model, but prefers to make them short and sharp. They are, it is true, sometimes *apparently* long; but, if we compare them with those of his contemporary, Clarendon, or with those of his predecessor, Hooker, we shall see that they are long only by courtesy of punctuation. The removal of a few conjunctions, or the insertion of a few full stops, is sufficient to make them simple

and brief. You do not need to take them to pieces
in order to understand them, nor have you to turn
over the page in order to find the main verb. He
studies the convenience of his readers, and, when
he thinks it desirable, calls on arithmetic to supply
the deficiencies of syntax: he divides his work into
short and numbered paragraphs, each of which is
summed up in a few terse and trenchant phrases;
while even within the paragraph a 1–2–3 helps us to
follow the order of his ideas. As a result, he is one
of the clearest of seventeenth-century writers; and
probably not till the time of Dryden do we light on
one who gives his reader so much solid thought at
the cost of so little trouble. Yet, in spite of the
dictum that easy writing makes hard reading, there
is no sign that he spent much pains over the details
of composition. There are repetitions, confusions,
pleonasms, and other laxities, which, though not
annoying to the sympathetic student, betray a
certain haste and carelessness. He was a Caroline
Walter Scott, and was probably unable to write at
all if he did not write rapidly. Nevertheless, he is
almost always, as we have said, pellucid; and his
perspicuity is due to an inborn simplicity and order-
liness of mind: he thinks straightforwardly, and
writes as he thinks. For pure, vivid, unadorned, and
unostentatious English, I know few passages to sur-
pass the description of the coronation of Charles the
First, in the eleventh book of his *History*; a passage

to which a tinge of tragedy is added in the concluding words:

> I have insisted the longer on this subject, moved thereunto by this consideration—that if it be the last solemnity performed on an English King in this kind, posterity will conceive my pains well bestowed, because on the last. But if hereafter Divine Providence shall assign England another King, though the transactions herein be not wholly precedential, something of state may be chosen out grateful for imitation.

As with every author, of course, due appreciation is possible only on the condition that we gain an understanding of his circumstances and of his mental equipment. And here we are ourselves to blame if we cannot meet him on his own ground. The history of his times is within reach of all; and the basis of his style is still closer at hand. The core of Fuller's learning, which was wide and deep, and the material of his wit, which is unsurpassed, was the Bible. Like the works of Hall, Bunyan, Chillingworth, and, in fact, almost all the great writers of the age, of every school, his works are a tissue of biblical phraseology. He lives in Scripture, argues from what it contains and from what it omits; quotes it at every turn, alludes to it, forms his style on it. And he expects from his readers something of the same familiarity. When he notes that four cities claim the bones of St Alban, he compares the saint to the river of Paradise; as that had four heads, so Alban must have had four bodies. Observing how many early saints were, or were said to be, of royal lineage, he remarks that the Jews make Ruth the daughter of Eglon, King of Moab, that the descent of David may be the more illustrious. Writing to James Hay, Earl of Carlisle, he compares the famous exploit of his ploughman ancestor, who routed the Danes at Loncarty with a yoke, to the victory of Eleazar, the son of Dodo, in the barley-plot. "Be not ashamed," he adds, "of the ploughman's yoke in your coat of arms; for it is probable that the posterity of Shamgar gave the goad for their hereditary ensign." King Oswald fell at Heaven's Field, a name that did not become appropriate till that time. "So," says Fuller, "Onesimus (useful) and Eutychus (fortunate) were so called from their infancy, but never truly answered to their names till after the conversion of the one and reviving of the other." He loves his Bible so much, indeed, that he plays and jests with it. When Augustine baptised ten thousand in one day, he is said to have made them go into the river two by two and baptise one another; "otherwise Joshua's day, when the sun stood still, had been too short for one man's personal performance of such an employment." Dunstan's celebrated miracle at Calne he compares sarcastically with Samson's crowning achievement; for while the hero could not pull down the temple on the Philistines without killing himself, the saint so contrived matters as to destroy his adversaries and spare his friends. Fuller has, in fact, a biblical parallel ready for nearly every incident he records; and, if wit lies in the perception of obscure likenesses between things apparently dissimilar, not Bacon himself has more wit than he.

All this, as was not surprising, brought on him the censure of dullards, both in his own time and later, to whom this light treatment of sacred things seemed little removed from blasphemy. Some who were not dullards attacked it for reasons of their own. The sarcastic South, to whom Fuller, with his moderate churchmanship, appeared no better than a Puritan, chose this characteristic as one of his chief pretexts for laying on the lash of invective; though assuredly he would have found no fault with a Non-juror who had offended in a like fashion. But the habit was so natural to Fuller that he was almost unconscious of it. When assailed for it by Peter Heylin—who, indeed, was the last man to throw stones on such an account—he answered, in his *Appeal of Injured Innocence*, "Let him at leisure produce the most light and ludicrous story in all my book, and here I stand ready to parallel it with as light, I will not say in the Animadvertor, but in as grave authors as ever put pen to paper." It is clear that the charge surprised him; he could not understand why love should not play with the objects of its affection. He agreed with Milton—a very different man—in holding that

joking decides great things
Stronger and better, oft, than earnest can:

what argument cannot do, jest may sometimes accomplish; nor is to use Holy Writ lightly the same thing as ridiculing it.

Rarely indeed, except where Papists, Pelagians, Arians, or Brownists are concerned, and by no means always even then, is the wit wanting in the saving grace of charity; rarely indeed is it barbed with malice. And how unerringly it hits the mark! What could be better than his saying that "some people sail to the port of their own praise by a side wind"? Or how could pious poetasters be more neatly hit off than in the words with which he describes Sternhold and Hopkins—"They had drunk more deeply of Jordan than of Helicon"?

Like most of his contemporaries, he does not disdain a pun; indeed to him, as to Shakespeare and the ancient Hebrews, a pun was a sort of newly discovered Eldorado, the knowledge of which it was almost a crime not to share with your fellows. Canting heraldry, of course, he loved, and would have appreciated the *Festina lente* of the Onslows. When dedicating a "century" of his *History* to Lord Dorchester, the head of the Pierrepoint family, he "craves leave to remind his lordship of that allusive motto to his name, *Pie repone te*"; nor is this by any means the only passage which would have made the Baron of Bradwardine throw down the book and take up his Titus Livius. But he puns on his own account. When criticising Geoffrey of Monmouth's statement that there were in ancient Britain twenty-eight cities having *flamens*, or pagan priests, of whom three were arch-flamens, he says that the flamens and arch-flamens were flams and arch-flams, even notorious falsehoods. The Saxon god Flynt (a deity unknown to Grimm and Muellenhoff) "was so termed because set on a flint-stone, which had more sparks of Divine nature than that idol which thereon was erected." Whether the derivation, which he cannot help giving, though he inclines to reject it, of Tyburn from *tie* and *burn*, because the victim was tied by the neck and burnt in the feet, be rather an example of the fantastic etymologies prevalent at the time than strictly a pun, is a question we leave to the discretion of the reader.

At times his jests are of a still lighter consistency than mere verbal plays; they are but the froth on the surface of his effervescing mind, unstudied and irrepressible scintillations from a lamp always alight. Speaking of the British birth of Constantine, he says that "certain authors softly rock the cradle of (*yet little*) Constantine the Great." In the dedication of the Third Century to Mr Simeon Bonnell, merchant, who seems to have resembled Zacchaeus both in wealth and in inches, he remarks, "It is proportionable to present a century, short in story, to one low in stature though deservedly high in esteem." Matthew of Westminster, surnamed Florilegus, "cropped a weed instead of a flower" when he perpetrated an historical error. *Hector* Boece and *Polydore* Virgil, bearing the names of two sons of Priam, take the liberty of giving us Homeric fictions instead of fact. The great Roman Wall, though of stone, was of no use against the Picts when manned with "stocks." When relating the legend that Merlin conjured the cromlechs of Stonehenge from Ireland through the sky, Fuller must needs suggest that they came in Charles's Wain. In fact, as the man in *Hudibras* did ne'er open his mouth but a trope flew out, so Fuller, if he descries but the most distant promise of a *jeu de mots*, cannot help greeting it from afar. He seems to have made an agreement with the nymph Euphrosyne to keep him everlastingly supplied with quips, cranks, and wanton wiles.

His memory is as quick as his invention; for we doubt if any work of equal length, with the single exception of *Don Quixote*, contains such a multitude of proverbs as does the *Church History*; but where the common store fails him, he has, like Mrs Poyser, the gift of forging them for himself. Probably it would be hard in many cases to decide whether they are borrowed or made for the occasion. The mind of Fuller was such a mirror of the best popular mind of the time that he was quite capable at a moment's notice of informing "the wisdom of many with the wit of one." "God never sends His servants on a

sleeveless errand"—is this his own, or taken from
the national stock? "Victorious bays bear only
barren berries"—a saying the truth of which was
never clearer than to-day—sounds like a common
saw, but may be only another of Fuller's skilful
coinages. "Light leaves are wagged with little
wind"; "Who would not entitle themselves to the
honour of martyrdom when parted from the pain?";
"That bowl which lies next the mark has most take
aim to remove it"; "The swaying of David's sceptre
did not hinder the tuning of his harp"; "Men may
make clothes either for mirth or for mourning"—
these are sayings—many of them pointed with an
alliteration in the good old Teutonic style—which,
like some of Bacon's, if they are not proverbs ought
to be: and they are but two or three out of hundreds
that stud the works of Fuller.

But all this, alone, would fail to explain his
peculiar charm. There is much besides, and of a
higher cast; a humanity rare in that age and not too
common in ours; a liberality and freedom from
bigotry remarkable in a man of strong and definite
views—easily mimicked but not so easily reproduced in a century distinguished more by indifference than by true tolerance—boldness in the expression of opinion at a time when opinions were often
crimes; an Herodotean love of good stories, which,
like Herodotus, he frequently tells with a *caveat*; a
genuine learning, which constantly breaks through

the veil of modesty and liveliness; and, finally, an engaging candour which never hesitates to own mistake. That his charity sometimes fails we have already noted; he has the good churchman's dislike of heresy. If it fails also, now and then, in his dealings with the Catholics, this shows merely that he was the man of his age and country; he stumbles where the authors of *Areopagitica* and of the *Letters on Toleration* stumbled just before and just after him. But it remains true, as Coleridge said, that he was "the least prejudiced great man in an age that boasted a galaxy of great men." That he could recognise goodness wherever it arose is made plain by his account of Abbot Feckenham, who,

like the axle-tree, stood firm and fixed in his own judgment, while the times, like the wheels, turned backwards and forwards round about him. He applied himself to Bonner, where he crossed the proverb "Like master, like man," the patron being cruel, the chaplain kind, to such who in judgment dissented from him. He never dissembled his religion, and under King Edward VI suffered much for his conscience. In the reign of Queen Mary he was wholly employed in doing good offices for the afflicted Protestants, from the highest to the lowest. The Earl of Bedford tasted of his kindness; so did Sir John Cheke; yea, and the Lady Elizabeth herself, who...coming to the crown, as some have confidently guessed, offered him the Archbishopric of Canterbury, on condition he would conform to her laws; which he utterly refused. In the treaty between the Protestants and Papists... his judgment was asked with respect and heard with reverence, his moderation being much commended.

Conversely, Fuller refuses to whitewash a Protestant simply on account of his Protestantism. When he comes to discuss the martyrdom of Sir John Oldcastle, finding himself much "intricated" by the conflicting accounts handed down of that enigmatical character, he declines the post of judge. "If my hand were put on the Bible, I should take it back again, yet so that, as I will not acquit, I will not condemn him, but leave all to the last day of the revelation of the righteous judgment of God." Even the authority of Foxe could not avail with him against the truth.

He knew the difference between the important and the trivial. Much as he hated heresy, he could not bring himself to think that Aidan and Columba ought to be censured for their ideas as to the correct date of Easter; and, with all his reverence for Bede, he thinks him a little pettifogging in making so much of the matter. After all, as it was but a dispute about moons, he regards Beza as right in dismissing it as a *lunatica quaestio*: welcoming the pun with none the less enthusiasm that it is not his own.

His humanity is revealed by slight touches everywhere. He will not, it is true, satisfy the opponents of capital punishment: the book of Genesis declares, "Whoso sheddeth man's blood, by man shall his blood be shed"; and in the palmy days of verbal inspiration a text had to be taken as it stood. But

note a certain gentleness, beyond that of the time,
peeping out in the midst of his narrative of the death
of John Scotus Erigena:

> Pouring learning into his lads (rather in proportion to the
> plenty of the fountain than to the receipt of the vessels), he
> was severe to such scholars as were dull in their apprehensions.
> This so irritated their anger against him, that by a universal
> conspiracy they dispatched him in the school with their pen-
> knives. I find not what punishment was inflicted upon them,
> whipping being too little, if sturdy youths, and hanging too
> much, if but little boys.

It is characteristic of him that, after telling the
legend, he hints pretty clearly that he does not believe
it; pointing out, from the stores of his knowledge,
that Prudentius had told the same tale, centuries
before, of the death of Cassian.

His candour appears, perhaps, most clearly in his
controversy with Heylin. The episode is somewhat
amusing. Having spoken of Cricklade and Lechlade
as ancient seats of learning, and having alluded to
the supposed derivation of the names from Greek-
lade and Latinlade respectively—such was the philo-
logy of the seventeenth century!—he came under
the correction of Heylin, who asserted that Lechlade
means the place of leeches or doctors, and that
Latten, a tiny village near by, was the real abode of
Latin study. Fuller accepted the "animadversion."
"My next edition," said he, "shall be reformed
accordingly." But still more quaintly is the same

quality shown whenever he has to speak of Oxford and Cambridge. A loyal son of no fewer than three Cambridge colleges, he was the author of a history of his University, and, as is well known, accepts the most amazing stories as to her antiquity. Even Sigebert's legendary foundation of the school in 631 ("but some make it four years after," he adds sadly) is not early enough for him. "She has more ancient titles to learning, which she deriveth, according to good authors, from many hundred years before." And, though his historical sense leads him to doubt whether these "good authors" are altogether to be relied on, the eternal undergraduate in him longs, sentimentally, to believe them.

All such things in either University, though specious to the eye, must be closely kept, and tenderly touched, lest, being roughly handled, they should moulder into dust. Let none suspect my extraction from Cambridge will betray me into partiality to my mother, who desire in this difference to be like Melchizedek, without descent, only to be directed by the truth. And here I make this fair and free confession, which I hope will be accepted for ingenuous: that as in Tamar's travail of twins Zerah first put out his hand, and then drew it in again, whilst Perez first came forth into the world, so I plainly perceive Cambridge with an extended arm, time out of mind, first challenging the birthright and priority of place for learning, but afterwards, drawing it in again, she lay for many years desolate, whilst Oxford, if later, larger, came forth in more entire proportion, and ever since constantly continued in the full dimensions of a University.

It is in the same liberal spirit that, when recording the old tradition that Alfred was the founder of University College, Oxford, he says, "Yet some say, Alfred did *find* and not *found* letters therein"; so that even Oxford may, if she desires, seek her origin in the mists of the remote past.

As for Fuller's boldness in the expression of opinion, it was such that some have thought the Government of the Protector must have given him, as a sort of cheerful Jaques, as large a charter as the wind, to blow on whom he pleased. The book opens with a patent allusion to the times, of the kind which few despotic monarchies would have permitted: "I shall not wonder that good men die so soon, but that they live so long, seeing wicked men desire their room here on earth, and God their company in heaven"; and he speaks of his intention of surrounding his dedication with black, as a "fitting emblem of the present condition of our distracted Church." One might fix the date of his history by the words, "when England sank from a kingdom to a state"; and there are to be found constant thinly veiled sarcasms on the political situation of the time. Yet Cromwell gave him a license to preach, and passed by all these attacks without notice: a clear proof, had Fuller been willing to admit it, that things were better than they had been under Laud, or than they were to be under Sheldon. No licenser appears to have considered the question of sup-

pressing the *History* as Tomkins all but suppressed
Paradise Lost. To us, for whom the controversies
of 1655 are as dead as the Crusades, these daring
innuendoes do but add a little spice to a work that
hardly needs it.

viii

But al shal passe that men prose or ryme,
Take every man his turn, as for his tyme.
                    CHAUCER, *Envoy to Scogan.*

WHEN Job cried, "Why do the wicked live,
grow old, wax mighty in power?" he was
putting a question the answer to which was scarcely
even conceivable until the doctrine of another life,
in which the inequalities of this world should be
remedied, broke upon the Jewish theological vision.
So long as the view was held that prosperity in
this life implied godliness, there was an inevitable
conflict between the conclusions of theory and the
witness of experience. A similar question might be
raised in a sphere with which morality and worldly
success have nothing to do: the sphere of literature.
"Why do certain poets gain fame, grow old in glory,
and wax mighty in popularity?" Here again recourse is had by some to the doctrine of a future
life. A later age will put things right: the bad poets
will be condemned to the Tartarus of oblivion, and
the good will be called up to the heaven of remembrance.

But even thus the question can hardly be settled.
It is, in one way, easy to account for the worldly
prosperity of the wicked: they aim at it, and they

are far better suited to attain it than the good. A certain lack of scruple is, if not essential, yet very useful in the chase after material success, and an honest grocer is at an obvious disadvantage in competing with his unhampered rival. But the bad poet and the good are seeking the same ends; and, in the strict sense of the word, cheating is impossible. Both alike must be open and above-board: both alike appear with their samples of verse, samples which cannot be privily adulterated. If we are taken in, it is our own fault, and ours only. The merits or defects of poetry may, it is true, lie below the surface; but we are at liberty to unpack and analyse to any extent we please: nor is it in the author's power to hide them. And yet in how many hundreds of cases has the public allowed itself to be deceived! How often has the poet's own generation—to say nothing of posterity—annulled the first judgment, and recalled the acclamations it has itself bestowed! No one compelled it to acclaim in the first instance; no one, to speak fairly, deluded it into acclaiming: why did it make the mistake, and—what is often as hard to understand—why did it correct it?

On the other hand, we have little security that the second trial is any more just than the first. It is often quite as hasty, and the decision is often given on quite irrelevant grounds. Nor, even if the pretender is, as sometimes happens, deposed, is there any guarantee that the rightful heir is enthroned:

too frequently the one usurper but gives place to another. What reason, indeed, have we to imagine that the future will be more competent than the present? Like us, it has dimensions and passions, and will be subject to disturbing influences. Reaction is no more likely to be right than action, and the pendulum of opinion swings to and fro for ever, none of its positions being more permanent than any other.

At the same time, there is an interest in watching these variations of taste, and in trying to decide why a poet is popular at one epoch and despised at another. Things do not happen without causes: if Bavius and Maevius had admirers, there must have been *something* in them that, if not exactly worthy of admiration, tended to rouse it. Nor does their subsequent oblivion in the least prove that they were bad: it may be a mere accident—as some bad poets have certainly survived and some good ones have been forgotten—or it may be that they were not quite adapted to a changed, but not necessarily improved, taste.

An instructive case well within living memory, of a poet thus, like a coward, dying before his death, is that of Stephen Phillips. At first acclaimed as a second Milton, he maintained his position for perhaps ten years, and then, like Milton's Satan, fell utterly and irretrievably. With a gross want both of fairness and of logic, the people resented their

own mistake, and seemed to take it as a crime in
Phillips that they had thought well of him: they
punished him simply because they had exalted him,
and damned him for their own too lavish praise.
Yet it is quite a tenable view that Phillips, though
not a great poet, was not a bad one: there are worse
poems than *Marpessa* which are still remembered,
and worse plays than *Paolo and Francesca* which are
still acted. This, however, is not our present point.
What we are inquiring is why, if Phillips does not
deserve remembrance, he was ever known. What
was the quality in him which secured him his great
popularity, but which could not secure him a lasting
repute? It is not as if he took advantage of some
ephemeral emotion: his poems are all on great and
universal topics, and *in appeal* are as wide as the
Iliad itself. One can understand why Brown's *Esti-
mate*, evoked by the peculiar circumstances of 1756,
should "rise like a paper kite and charm the town,"
to fall like a kite when the national fortunes altered:
but *Christ in Hades* is scarcely a theme to vary with
a change of social or political opinion.

More remarkable still, perhaps, is the case of
Philip James Bailey. There can, I think, be no doubt
that Bailey was a true, and almost a great, poet. His
poem gained the suffrages, not of a chorus of indolent
reviewers, but of Tennyson, Browning, and Ruskin,
not of playgoers who could not distinguish between
the dramatist and the actor or the scene-shifter,

but of men of sound and balanced judgment. The eleven editions of *Festus* were purchased by discriminating readers, not in a rush of wild enthusiasm, but during a space of fifty years—a space in which, assuredly, an impostor ought to have been detected. Yet when, in 1902, I attended Bailey's funeral, I noticed everywhere signs that his was a glory that had waned; and since then it has been all but extinguished. And yet his work is as good now as it was in 1839: the thoughts are as applicable to present conditions as to those of Victoria's reign; the poem deals with questions which must always attract the thoughtful mind: why then, first, did it attain a vogue, and why, secondly, has it dropped out of notice?

I am not, it will be seen, here considering the L. E. L.'s, the Felicia Hemanses, the Martin Tuppers, nor even the Lewis Morrises; not the Eliza Cooks, the Lydia Sigourneys, the Charles Mackays, who once sold their scores of thousands, and now line bandboxes. Yet even here you have to explain why they got their readers. It is probable that Eliza Cook had, in her day, as many readers as Keats will have in his eternity: she had, so to speak, a *horizontal* immortality as great as Keats's *vertical*. This needs accounting for, as much as any other human phenomenon. For poets of her stamp, it is plain, won not only their own approbation but that of many others. I once read through Pollok's *Course of Time*—a

dreary desert, in whose six or seven thousand lines
there is perhaps but one that deserves to be remembered, that in which the sound Calvinism of the
author describes the future of a Prelatical Arminian,
who will face the Judgment

> Unfrocked, unbeneficed, uncorpulent:

for, apparently, like the olive in Jotham's fable, he
has to "leave his fatness." Yet I know a work, by a
writer of no contemptible ability, in which the *Course
of Time* is solemnly declared to have conferred a new
lustre on Holy Writ by turning so much of its prose
into blank verse: and few poems have, in their time,
been oftener quoted. Such a mystery cries aloud for
a solution.

Or, to go back a century before Pollok, what is
one to say of John Hughes, whose *Triumph of Peace*,
written in 1697 to celebrate the Treaty of Ryswick,
was received as one of the greatest works ever
written by a young man of twenty? "I think,"
wrote a "gentleman of Cambridge" to one of
Hughes's friends, soon after the verses appeared,

> I think I never heard a poem read with so much admiration
> as the *Triumph of Peace* was by our best critics here, nor a
> greater character given to a young poet at his first appear-
> ance; no, not even to Mr Congreve himself. So nobly ele-
> vated are his thoughts, his numbers so harmonious, and his
> turns so fine and delicate, that we cry out with Tully on a
> like occasion, Nostrae spes altera Romae.

And this in the last and best days of Dryden, as the

considered opinion of men familiar with the master-
pieces of Greece and Rome! To the reader of to-day,
the "thoughts" appear commonplace, the "numbers" monotonous, the "turns" obvious or clumsy,
and the whole poem but a fair specimen of the
occasional: no worse, but certainly no better, than
Boileau's on the capture of Namur or Addison's on
the victory of Blenheim; the sole interest, perhaps,
lying in the incidental allusion to St Paul's Cathe-
dral, the choir of which was opened on the day of
the thanksgiving for the Peace. As for the rest of
Hughes's two volumes, they are if possible duller
than his first performance: and yet the critics of the
time invariably speak of him as a genius. Addison,
indeed, went so far as to consult him about *Cato*:
and it is said—no great tribute, perhaps, in reality—
that the last act of that play owed much to Hughes's
assistance or encouragement.

Examples might easily be multiplied. I might, for
instance, mention Hayley, as bad poetically as he
was morally excellent, whose *Triumphs of Temper*
and other equally unreadable works were once read
with admiration by cultured and uncultured alike.
But I propose to confine myself to what is possibly
the most astonishing case of all, the case of a writer
who, for quite a considerable time, enjoyed a vast
popularity, which to us is more unaccountable than
that of any other we could adduce. John Pomfret
was born in 1667, ten years before Hughes. He was

a little later in gaining renown, but in 1699, at the age of thirty-two, produced a poem which threw the *Triumph of Peace* into the shade. This was *The Choice*: a poem which, says Johnson, was better known and more read than any other in the English language. Johnson, writing in 1780, when the vogue had ceased, is plainly puzzled by the poem's popularity. "In his poems is an easy volubility, the pleasure of smooth metre is offered to the ear, and the mind is not oppressed with ponderous nor entangled with intricate sentiment. He pleases many; and he who pleases many must have some species of merit." Faint praise: but Johnson was compelled, nevertheless, to admit Pomfret into his series, and in his *Lives of the Poets* allots him a perfunctory biography.

I have little doubt, moreover, that judges as good as Johnson had read Pomfret, and perhaps enjoyed him more. It seems more than possible that Goldsmith's famous couplet,

> The hawthorn bush, with seats beneath the shade,
> For talking age and whispering lovers made,

is an echo, conscious or unconscious, of *The Fortunate Complaint*:

> As Strephon, in a withered cypress shade,
> For anxious thought and sighing lovers made:

and the unintentionally amusing preface to the poems of 1699 may have given a hint to Pope:

> To please everyone would be a new thing, and to write so as to please nobody would be as new; for even Quarles and

Wythers (*sic*) have their admirers. The Author is not so fond of fame to desire it from the injudicious many, nor of so mortified a temper not to wish it from the discerning few. It is not the multitude of applauses, but the good sense of the applauders, which establishes a valuable reputation; and if a Rymer or a Congreve say it is well, he will not be at all solicitous how great the majority may be to the contrary.

Nothing could easily be more humorous than to see the author of *The Choice* following the author of *Paradise Lost* in hoping for a fit audience though few; unless it be his expectation of immortality from gaining the suffrages of a critic like Rymer, whose one claim to remembrance is that he abused Shakespeare. Incidentally, also, the contemptuous allusion to Quarles and Wither is an illustration of the instability of literary judgments; for these two were during half a century the ready and constant types of bad poets. Yet in the voluminous works of Quarles there are many inspired passages; and Wither, though he wrote too much, wrote also some of the most exquisite lyrics in the English language. It is true that Pomfret had probably never read a line of either; yet his tone of airy superiority is none the less exquisitely ludicrous.

The poems thus introduced gained exactly the audience the writer professed not to wish: unfit, though many. No poem, as we have seen, was oftener read than *The Choice*; and Johnson, who notes this extraordinary popularity, was writing when Gray's *Elegy* had already been thirty years before the world. We may then give this poem a life of threescore years and ten—a life far longer than some very excellent performances have achieved, and representing a number of readers larger than some of the greatest poets, in all probability, ever will touch. To study this poem, then, will give us some idea not only of the author, but—what is more important—of the readers to whom it appealed; and, human nature being always pretty much the same, it may help an ambitious versifier of our own day to attain a similar renown. *Mutatis mutandis*, a poet who does in 1930 what Pomfret did in 1700 will succeed like him.

In the first place, we notice that the poem has scarcely one atom of originality. As Johnson says, it "exhibits a system of life adapted to common notions and equal to common expectations; such a state as affords plenty and tranquillity, without exclusion of intellectual pleasures." It has, for this reason, "been always the favourite of that class of readers who, without vanity or criticism, seek only their own amusement[1]." The gist of it may be found in the prayer of Agur the son of Jakeh, "Give me neither poverty nor riches"; and there is no reason to think that the sentiment was new even in Agur's

---

[1] *Amusement* in the proper sense of the word, which it retained till the middle of the last century: that of *interest*, without any necessary notion of the witty or humorous.

time. But Pomfret makes very little attempt, by freshness of setting, to hide the antiquity of the thought. His ornaments and illustrations are practically all borrowed, and not from very recondite sources. Like Horace, he wishes for a seat neither too small nor too large; not omitting the *hortus*, the *iugis aquae fons*, or the *paullum silvae*:

> A little garden, grateful to the eye,
> And a cool rivulet run murmuring by,
> On whose delicious banks a stately row
> Of shady limes or sycamores should grow.

Like Horace also, though careful to substitute "Heaven" for "Maia nate," he utters the prayer that these gifts may be lasting—"propria ut mihi munera faxis." It is also pretty plain that Pomfret stole a glance at one of the most familiar epigrams of Martial. If Martial desires *lis nunquam, sine arte mensa, nox non ebria sed soluta curis*, the Englishman would "shun lawsuits with studious care," "a frugal plenty should his table spread," and he would have a small but well-stored wine-cellar:

> Wine whets the wit, improves its native force,
> And gives a pleasant flavour to discourse;
> By making all our spirits debonair,
> Throws off the lees, the sediment of care.

But his chief storehouse is Cowley, that abundant poet from whom so many, from Pope to Patmore, have borrowed so freely. *The Choice*, in fact, is but Cowley's *Wish* over again, with certain omissions

here and expansions there. Cowley, it is true, had
Horace and Martial in his mind, and all but verbally
translates a line from the latter: "I would not fear
nor wish my fate"—"Summum nec metuas diem,
nec optes": but he imitates with the originality of
a true poet. Pomfret, on the other hand, when
he steals, spoils in the stealing by diffuseness and
didacticism. Thus Cowley says,

> Acquaintance I would have, but when 't depends
> Not on the number, but the choice of friends.

Pomfret expands these two lines into two pages.
"Books should, not business, entertain the light,"
says Cowley; Pomfret gives us twenty lines, ending
sententiously enough,

> In some of these, as Fancy should advise,
> I'd always take my morning exercise;
> For sure no minutes bring us more content
> Than those in pleasing useful studies spent.

"This only grant me, that my means may lie too
low for envy, for contempt too high," says Cowley:
the corresponding passage in Pomfret runs off into
a sermon: and the result is that though his poem
numbers but a hundred and sixty lines, it is too
long by a hundred.

It would appear, then, that one main condition
of a great, if ephemeral, popularity is to take common thoughts, illustrate them with simple images
which have already been proved and tested by others,

develop these, or rather thin them out, at a certain not too wearisome length, and add a sprinkling of homiletics. And we are confirmed in this view by noticing how many of the most popular "poets" of this and other times have thus adopted ordinary ideas, illustrated them on familiar lines, and attenuated the thread of their discourse until no mental effort is necessary in order to understand it: taking care, by an infusion of mild piety, to make the poem innocuous and improving in its tendency. Many of our recent aspirants have made the mistake of being violent, novel, or daring: they contort themselves like would-be Sibyls, try to pose as original, and flout the accepted codes of morality. They are wrong: the real way to gain a hearing is to be orthodox, imitative, and timidly unobtrusive.

We notice, secondly, that the poem is written in the manner and metre most approved by the time. The age was the age of Dryden. The last fifty years had seen the victory of the style introduced by Waller and Denham, the smooth monotonous couplet, into which, it is true, the Laureate had infused energy and virility, but which lent itself naturally to the presentation of mild ideas in a pleasing fashion. This verse is of exactly the kind to make prose seem like poetry, and to give an appearance of originality to what, if unrhymed, would attract no attention. The ordinary reader, seeing his own ideas rendered in a tepidly epigrammatic form, fancies them fine: precisely as the hearer of a Tillotson, listening to everyday thoughts neatly and charmingly linked in well-sounding sentences, fancied he was being stirred and informed when he was only being soothed. The reader of Pomfret, similarly, familiar with the rhythm and the diction, receives exactly the impression he expects; he is neither startled nor distracted, but quietly beguiled into imagining that he is thinking. The following passage, for example, might—apart from the preaching tone which made it yet more welcome—have come straight out of Denham or from one of Dryden's weaker and more perfunctory pieces:

> That life might be more comfortable yet,
> And all my joys refined, sincere, and great,
> I'd chuse two friends, whose company would be
> A great advance to my felicity:
> Airy and prudent; merry, but not light;
> Quick in discerning, and in judging right;
> Secret they should be, faithful to their trust,
> In reas'ning cool, strong, temperate, and just;
> Obliging, open, without huffing brave,
> Brisk in gay talking, and in sober grave;
> Not prone to lust, revenge, or envious hate,
> Nor busy meddlers with affairs of state;
> Strangers to slander, and sworn foes to spite,
> Not quarrelsome, but stout enough to fight;
> Loyal and pious, friends to Caesar; true,
> As dying martyrs, to their Maker too:
> In their society I could not miss
> A permanent, sincere, substantial, bliss.

This is a pleasant expansion of the two words of Martial, "pares amici," and of the two lines of Cowley quoted above. The writer does the reader's thinking for him, at the expense of a little tautology; and the reader is gratified in consequence. When we see our own ideas neatly expressed, in a not too difficult dialect which yet appears to raise them to a higher power, we cannot but be flattered and gently titillated. Observe also that the opinions are studiously moderate, adapted to those of the average man. Pomfret, says his biographer, was "far from being in the least tinctured with fanaticism": and nothing caused him more pain than being confused with a certain Dissenting teacher, Samuel Pomfret by name, of whose "destructive tenets" he often expressed his abhorrence. His verse, like his life, steered an even course in the *Via Media* of the Church, as far removed from Rome on the one hand as from Geneva on the other. He understood the British love of compromise, and knew that the mean is golden.

We should, then, advise the seeker after popularity to avoid all revolutionary utterances, and to choose as his medium of expression not some measure surprising and new, but one consecrated and fully perfected by the leading writers of the time; it is easier both for author and for reader to mimic an established form than to strike out a line of one's own. Modern writers of *vers libres*, and searchers after untried forms of versification, might lay the success of Pomfret to heart; recalling also the advice of Coleridge to the youthful Tennyson, to write in none but one or two well-known and strictly defined metres. The truly great public—whatever may be the case with reviewers—distrusts the odd.

A sound, but not too ostentatious piety, is also to be recommended. Despite of gods, men, and columns, the mediocre poet is sure of a certain circulation provided he puts in here and there a safe and orthodox paraphrase of Scripture, or an exhortation to a devout and decorous life. Among Pomfret's other poems are several "Pindaric Essays," dealing with the prospect of death, the Divine Attributes, and the General Conflagration that is to precede the Last Judgment: poems in which the "Pindaricism" was excused on account of the piety. There is also the *Lament of Eleaʒar over Jerusalem*, paraphrased, or rather elongated, out of Josephus; and *Dies Novissima*, or the *Last Epiphany*, entitled, for some reason, a Pindaric Ode rather than an Essay. All these were highly esteemed. In those days, at any rate, whatever the apparent greatness of a wanton bard, no one seems to have doubted that the moral bards were *ipso facto* of a higher class. Here the authority of Lord Halifax, the universal patron of the Muses, is without appeal. Writing to Hughes, and congratulating him on the purity of his verses, Halifax adds,

In all times, and in all ages of the world, the moral poets have been ever the greatest, and as much superior to others in wit as in virtue: nor does this seem difficult to be accounted for, since the dignity of their subjects naturally raised their ideas, and gave a grandeur to their sentiments.

He seems to have thought that the superiority of Virgil to Ovid, and of Milton to Dryden, consisted solely in a loftier morality. But Halifax, who probably paid more for poetry than any other man that ever lived, knew what he was talking about. We therefore fearlessly recommend those who are now beginning the ascent of Parnassus, to discard the clogs of irreligion and immorality, and devote their attention to sacred themes.

But lastly, there is one feature in which Pomfret does reveal a certain originality; and to this, we doubt not, he owed a vast increase of circulation. *The Choice* contains a long and elaborate compliment to women, which, when compared with the scarcely veiled contempt of Pope, and with the general opinion of the time, will be found truly remarkable, and is in many respects the most pleasing portion of the poem. As Dr Johnson found even the delights of driving in a chaise not quite complete without the company of a woman, so to Pomfret books, wine, a competent fortune, and a couple of discreet male friends are not enough unless Providence permits him

> Near some obliging modest fair to live;
> For there's that sweetness in a female mind
> Which in a man's we cannot hope to find.

Note that the "obliging fair" is not to be his wife; for Pomfret excluded marriage from his list of essentials to happiness; indeed so strongly does he insist on the necessity of bachelordom that Bishop Compton, thinking he meant to recommend the clergy to form irregular attachments, for some time refused to give him a living—and that though Pomfret, having altered his views, was then married.

But the description of the "fair" is none the less interesting; and, if the poet had a living model in his mind, may well serve to correct certain superficial judgments as to the character and accomplishments of Revolution women. "Who," he cries, "would so much satisfaction lose as witty nymphs in conversation give?" The whole passage, apart from the diction, might have been written by John Stuart Mill about his future wife:

> I'd have her reason all her passion sway,
> Easy in company, in private gay;
> Coy to the fop, to the deserving free,
> Still constant to herself, and just to me:
> A soul she should have, for great actions fit,
> Prudence and wisdom to direct her wit;
> Courage to look bold Danger in the face,
> No fear, but only to be proud or base;
> Quick to advise, by an emergence prest,
> To give good counsel, or to take the best;
> So faithful to her friend, and good to all,
> No censure might upon her actions fall.

To this fair creature he would from time to time

resort, to get from her conversation a new joy, and to find freedom from surly cares. Yet here, too, Pomfret shows his dread of "fanaticism." Even this pleasure must be taken in moderation:

> For highest cordials all their virtues lose
> By a too frequent or too bold a use;
> And what would cheer the spirits in distress
> Ruins our health when taken to excess.

Still, though women may have perhaps thought that Pomfret showed an exaggerated caution, and that he seemed to regard a woman as one of those good things of which it is perilously easy to have too much, there can, I think, be little doubt that they read the lines with pleasure, and that a large proportion of Pomfret's wide audience was to be found among those who saw their own image in the portrait of the "witty nymph."

We therefore fearlessly recommend those poets who desire a wide and speedily attained popularity, to write their poems, as Homer was said to have composed his *Odyssey*, for women.

ix

THE "ODE TO DUTY"

"Unde hanc homo arripuit?" ut ait apud Xenophontem Socrates.
De Natura Deorum, Bk. ii, cap. vi.

ORIGINALITY, as has been well said, is not mere novelty. When Ecclesiastes remarked that there was no new thing under the sun, he was at the very same time himself producing a work of high originality, and saying something old in a new way. Superficially regarded, everything modern is ancient, and the thing that hath been is that which shall be: the sun is wearied with the sameness of that which goes on under it. Every inventor has had his predecessor, and the utmost he can claim is that he has changed the form of that which, in another shape, existed before. Nay, the sun himself, says Timon, is a thief who robs the vast sea; but the sea itself has robbed the moon, who in her turn is living on stolen light. And so with literature. The most independent of writers, in this aspect, is a plagiarist, and the germ of every one of his ideas is to be found among the ideas of someone else. Even Swift, who boasted that nothing in him was not his own, has been detected in a thousand thefts, and the most immortal of poets has gained his immortality by borrowing from the dead.

Yet there is of course another side to all this. We know the original writer when we see him; and there remains a difference between the mere pilferer and the man who makes his own that which he has stolen. When Virgil was accused of robbing Homer, he answered his detractors by saying, "*You* could as easily rob Hercules of his club as rob Homer of a single line"; and the defence is sound. There are hundreds of lines from the *Iliad* in the *Aeneid*; yet every one of them is by Virgil.

Nevertheless, there is a pleasure and a use in tracing the "originals" of such borrowings, and in noting, as accurately as we can, how the borrower has *made* them his own. Such an investigation is not mere curiosity; it is an endeavour to penetrate into a great mind and to mark its workings: and no exercise can be more beneficial to lesser men, provided it be cautious, modest, and restrained. In this paper we propose just such an exercise for ourselves and our readers, applying our modest efforts to the study of a poem whose originality is beyond dispute.

No poet, in fact, is more self-sufficient than Wordsworth; and his individuality has been the theme of all his admirers from Coleridge down. This independence, indeed, cannot be missed by anyone who knows the state of literature at the moment when Wordsworth arose: more than almost any other poet, he struck out new paths and left the old. But this does not mean that he stands utterly alone, that you cannot see in the past that he disdained the germs of the work he set out to do. No more in his case than in that of others does it mean that he does not borrow, that he is a solitary miracle, or that he does not take his place in the natural succession of English poetry. "What he thinks he may require" he takes from those who have gone before him, and he adapts to his use thoughts from all and sundry. He is no poetic Melchizedek, without father and without mother, any more than he is without descent. The common fancy that he was little of a reader was always an unpardonable delusion, and has, one may hope, received the *coup de grâce* from Mr de Selincourt in his monumental edition of the *Prelude*[1]. He borrowed innumerable books from Southey and Coleridge, and *sometimes* returned them. His days were passed not only in communion with a living Nature, but in converse with the dead, by whose side he hoped to "travel on through all futurity"; and he was fully conscious of the work they had done and of the supplement he desired to make to it. Few men, not professed students, have known the whole range of English poetry better. He had, it is true, a remarkable power of rejecting what he could not readily assimilate; but what suited him simmered in his mind, and came forth at last,

---

[1] It is true that in his rigid *later* years he read little except his own poems: but in his youth it was not so.

like the stores of the treasury of the scribes, a blend of new and old.

Thus, not merely in such obvious transmutations of ancient ideas as *Laodamia* and *Dion*, but in such poems as *Nutting* or the *Prelude* itself we light on Wordsworthian settings of common thoughts—original, not because they were never thought before, but because they have passed through a powerful mind. They are, in their fashion, like the borrowings of Virgil or Milton—not thefts, but assimilations. More than this we cannot ask from anyone.

But sometimes the conveying is more direct. Wordsworth has been reading, and we can see in his work the traces of the very book that has engaged his attention; he has been talking, perhaps to Coleridge, and we can see what the talk has been about. He is giving what he has received, transformed into poetry but otherwise almost unchanged: these thoughts have not, like others, come from he knows not where, and subconsciously moulded themselves he knows not how, to emerge as pure Wordsworth: they still retain the character of the rock from whence they were hewn, and some marks of the pit whence they were digged. It is then that we have, not what is commonly called the "original" Wordsworth, but Wordsworth the student; always, it is true, bringing to his reading "an understanding equal or superior," always haughty and dominant; but not the Wordsworth whose inspiration has come from the starry sky and the lonely hills. The thoughts are *accepted* thoughts; he holds them, and with conviction; they are his, but they are not *himself.*

Such a poem is the *Ode to Duty*—a poem often heedlessly taken as part and parcel of the true Wordsworth. To us, however, it seems to belong to the second class. The hints that gave rise to it appear to us open and palpable: Wordsworth is recollecting, more or less deliberately and consciously, not creating from an uncontrollable impulse. He is a messenger, not a seer; he is not in the high hour of visitation, but, as his own perhaps pedantic title-page has it, in the stage of "sentiment and reflection." Hence, as he never is when on fire, he is sometimes wrong.

This may seem a hard saying, and, to those "glad hearts" that love without analysing, it may be all but a blasphemy. In any case it needs defence; and defence shall be given: but first be it remembered that we shall say no word in *depreciation* of the poem. To botanise is not to love the flower less; and to put a poem in its exact place is no more to profane it than it is sacrilegious in a musician to set a sonata of Beethoven in relation to his other works. He may decide that the other works are truer or higher, but he none the less admires. Of some poems we can say "They came thus and thus": of others, only that the wind blew where it listed; but each kind, in its measure, claims our affection.

And first, let us look at the *form* of the poem. Here there is no doubt. It is that of Gray's *Hymn to Adversity*, in every detail; the same tetrameter quatrain, the same couplets, the same Alexandrine at the end: a ten-line stanza of no very common construction. The *tone* of the Ode, again, if we allow for a greater cheerfulness in the subject, is remarkably like that of the Hymn; it begins with a similar invocation, it passes through a similar phase of reflection, and ends on a similar personal note. The very phraseology is of the same cast: the one begins "Daughter of Jove, relentless Power"; the other, "Stern daughter of the voice of God." Wordsworth does indeed avoid Gray's besetting sin—the vice of over-personification; he has no long list of qualities with names duly begun with capitals, no Follies, Joys, Charities, or Pities; and he shuns also (not always with success) the peculiar eighteenth-century vocabulary. But we defy anyone with the smallest literary feeling to read the two poems in close succession without saying of the *Ode to Duty* what Lucretius said of the overthrow of superstition, "Primum Graius homo."

Having studied the Hymn, and having felt, through its reticence and somewhat stilted language, the really profound thought and true emotion that inform it—for Gray, though "he never spoke out," *had* strong emotions and could rouse them in his readers—Wordsworth would, more or less unconsciously, retain the poem in his mind as a form or mould; and into that mould, almost without effort, would fall such thoughts as occurred to him on a similar theme. Not more than the slightest hint would be necessary to start a train of suggestions: and we may conjecture that it was not long before that hint was given: either by reading or by some philosophic talk, nay, perhaps, by the mere recollection of some philosophic talk with Coleridge or another years before. The germ thus sown, the poem would spring forth all but unbidden; for the tune was given him already, and it needed but the words.

Such a germ he may have found by lighting on Kant's *Groundwork of the Metaphysic of Ethics*, or its sequel the *Critique of Practical Reason*. Let no one say that here is nothing to stir the poetic impulse. Kant himself was certainly no poet, but amid his "positions" and "corollaries" we can see the workings of a passion almost Shelleyan. Duty, says Kant, is the necessity of an act, arising out of the reverence for universal law; and, after spending many pages in elaborating this thesis, he suddenly bursts out into an apostrophe as startling as if Euclid, after demonstrating the *Pons Asinorum*, had suddenly soared into a lyric on its splendour and perfection. The mere word "Duty" acts like a spell, and turns him from a professor into a dithyrambist. True, the philosopher reasserts himself: but once more, as he concludes his somewhat arid treatise, the poet

returns: "Two things there are, which the oftener
and more steadfastly we contemplate them, fill the
mind with an ever new, ever rising wonder and
reverence, the starry heavens above and the moral
law within." It is these two things that Wordsworth's
Ode brings together.

But Kant, like Wordsworth, insists also on the
universal reign of duty: it binds not men only but
all thinking beings. "Ethics," he maintains, "is
valid for all Intelligents"; and it is on this account
that it is useless to seek its origin in human nature
merely. Duty rests on *reason*, and is a portion of
absolute and irrefragable truth: it belongs not to the
"phenomenal" but to the "noumenal" world, and
its "categorical imperatives" are without appeal even
for the gods themselves. Hence not only *must* we
obey its dictates, but we can rely on them with
unhesitating trust: "si fractus illabatur orbis, im-
pavidum ferient ruinae." The "thou shalt" of Duty
is as certain as the certainty of Being itself. In fact,
to use the phrases of Wordsworth, it is "victory and
law," and it gives us "the confidence of reason."

Yet again, it comes in Kant's way to discuss how
far those who do "right" *without* the sense of Duty
can be said to do right at all: and it is well known
that, while admitting the "blissful course" which
such natures hold, he allows them a far lower
place than would be given them by most thinkers.
Theirs is but the innocence of childhood: it is really

inconsistent with that absolute Freedom of the Will which is the privilege of every Intelligent. Duty, like sin, is not imputed where there is no law: and a man who acts "rightly" without the reverential recognition of law is no more truly moral than one who does "right" from motives of expediency. He has no chart to guide him, and at the first cross-road he will be bewildered.

Here, though the *suggestion* may have come from Kant, it is clear that Wordsworth, like most people, thinks Kant's position too rigid. There is a charm in *innocent* virtue which it is certain no poet, and least of all the author of the "Lucy" poems, can resist; and Wordsworth, both a poet and a follower of Nature, was certain to recognise a moral value in that which Kant denied to be morality at all. To do the work of Duty, and know it not, is something beautiful; and though Wordsworth recognises that the time may come when knowledge is necessary, he refuses to see no worth in it. He himself has been thus innocent, and he believes that *then* he was nearer Heaven than now. But when the innocence passes, as pass it must, he gives to Duty all that Kant would claim for her.

To Kant, then, the poem owes the sense of law —a power as "relentless" as Gray's Adversity herself, uncompromising and immovable. To Kant also is due the recognition of *reason* behind the mandate: that reason which, as Milton held, was "the law of law itself," and whose claims upon the *intellect* are incontrovertible, as on the soul they are compelling. To Kant again Wordsworth owed the true idea of freedom in bondage; not that "unchartered freedom" which he had loved in youth, but the willing subjection to a universal law which he had learned in maturity. As a child he had—so he fancied— girded himself and walked whither he listed; now, capable of quiet thought, he tires of that "unchartered freedom[1]," and *supplicates* to be a bondman, to be guided to the end by that form of Truth in activity which is Duty. But lastly, in a slight reaction from the logical rigour of Kant, he still looks back with a certain wistful longing to the days when Duty was unknown and undreamed of, but when the natural untaught impulse led along the straight road and through the narrow gate. Like Henry Vaughan, he longed for the early days when he shined in angel-infancy, before his soul could fancy anything but a white celestial thought.

There is, however, much more in the poem than Kantianism. No poet desires, or needs, to be a sternly consistent philosopher; and Wordsworth fearlessly mingles with the "critical" philosophy a good deal that is derived from the dogmatic system of Stoicism. It is not open to doubt that he must

---

[1] The *phrase*, of course, is suggested by Shakespeare: "The air, a chartered libertine, is still" (*Henry V*, I. i. 48); "I must have liberty, as large a charter as the wind," says Jaques (*As You Like It*, II. vii. 48). Wordsworth had thought himself *freer* than the wind.

have admired that system; his own temperament, though fortune made but slight call on him to put Stoical maxims into practice, was of the Stoic kind; and as for his friend Coleridge, to whom he owed so much, *his* enthusiasm for the Porch was almost unbounded. Desiring to express his feeling for St Paul, "The Epistle to the Romans," said Coleridge, "seems to me the most profound work in the world, and *I can hardly imagine the writings of the old Stoics to have been deeper.*" We do not know that Wordsworth read widely in Seneca, Marcus Aurelius, or Epictetus; but in this very poem there are indications that he knew *something* of them. The "repose that ever is the same" is the "ataraxia" of the Stoic slave, whose freedom in bondage may also have struck Wordsworth's imagination. But be this as it may, he must have known some of Cicero's philosophical dialogues. He may have observed in the *De Officiis*—a book in his day universally read at school or college—an indication that the Stoics, unlike Kant, attributed moral worth to the natural instincts of children, and he may have learnt that Stoicism, herein agreeing with Kantianism, considered the highest life to be that lived according to Reason—a Reason universalised, and pervading the whole world. Not improbably, also, he knew the stress laid by Stoicism on the necessity of conquering those "Phantasiai" which, in many respects, remind us of the "chance desires" of his Ode. But in particular he would read the *De Natura Deorum*, in which he would find, clearly and pleasantly explained, many doctrines singularly in harmony with his own ideas. The thought of Duty, its sovereignty and its universality, on which the Stoics insisted no less strongly than Kant himself, would inevitably call up recollections, more or less vague, of their theories; and these recollections, scarcely indeed perceived to be recollections, would fall easily and naturally into the given framework of his poem.

As against the Epicurean doctrines, which are championed in the first book of the *De Natura Deorum* by Velleius, the second book gives, by the mouth of Lucilius Balbus, a presentation of the Stoic view of the universe: and a large part of the book is devoted to "proving" that the universe is not only living but divine. The arguments are often crude enough, and seem to have been adopted to buttress a foregone conclusion. "The world is spherical; the sphere is the most perfect of figures; the world is therefore perfect; it is therefore divine": such is the syllogism quoted in all seriousness from Zeno. Or again, "The rational is higher than the irrational: there is nothing higher than the Universe: therefore the Universe is rational": a very good example of several logical fallacies in one. It is not likely that Wordsworth the thinker was taken in by these reasonings; it was open to him, for instance, to reply with Velleius that to him the cone or the cylinder was quite as "perfect" as the sphere. But for the purposes of Wordsworth the poet the demonstration might well appear cogent enough; and in any case he could not fail to be struck by the imposing array of vivid *examples* which Balbus adduced to illustrate his point, examples drawn not only from this lower earth but from "the starry heavens above." "Each has his place appointed, each his course[1]"; but to Balbus

most wonderful of all are those five stars, falsely called planets or "straying." For nothing "strays" that through all eternity keeps its motions constant and unerring. Saturn, the Greek Phaenon, now advancing, now delaying, never fails to finish his course in the allotted time: Jupiter, or Phaethon, passes through the twelve signs and returns at the predestined moment to whence he started. Venus never departs, whether going or returning, more than an exact number of degrees from the sun. Hanc igitur in stellis constantiam, hanc tantam tam variis cursibus in omni aeternitate convenientiam temporum *non possumus intellegere sine mente, ratione, consilio*: this precision and punctuality prove a mind. There is in heaven no chance, no rashness, no error, no vacillation, but on the contrary all is order, truth, reason, immutability: and he who says that this can be without mind is himself mindless.

When we remember that Wordsworth, like Kant, has identified Duty with Reason, we cannot be sur-

---

[1] Milton, *Paradise Lost*, III. 720: Milton, I think, like Wordsworth, had in mind *De Natura Deorum*, II. xxii. 57: "Omnis natura habet viam quandam et sectam quam sequatur." The usual rendering of *sectam* is "path," and thus Milton seems to have read it: but it is possible to take it as "rule" or "order": if Wordsworth so took it, the likelihood that he is here following Cicero becomes greater.

prised that he should have been impressed by the words of Lucilius, or that he should have translated them into his own immortal phrases:

> Thou dost preserve the stars from wrong,
> And the most ancient heavens, through thee,
> are fresh and strong [1].

But it was unnecessary for Wordsworth to seek outside poetry for an account of Stoicism. He could find its essential doctrines already enshrined in verse —the verse to which, possibly, Paul alluded in his speech to the Stoics and their rivals at Athens. Cleanthes, the successor of Zeno, had long before, in his Hymn to Zeus, expressed the thoughts of Lucilius:

> σοὶ δὴ πᾶς ὅδε κόσμος ἑλισσόμενος περὶ γαῖαν
> πείθεται, ᾗ κεν ἄγῃς, καὶ ἑκὼν ὑπὸ σεῖο κρατεῖται.
> Thee, unto whom alone we owe our birth,
> The heavens obey, that roll around the earth:
> E'en as thou guidest, so they follow still,
> And willingly submit them to thy will.

---

[1] There can, I think, be little doubt that at the back of Wordsworth's mind lay also some memory of the words of Ulysses on "Degree," to which we have drawn attention in another essay (*Troilus and Cressida*, I. iii. 90):

> "The heavens themselves, the planets, and this centre [the earth]
> Observe degree, priority, and place:...
> Sol...whose medicinable eye
> Corrects the ill aspects of planets evil,
> And posts like the commandment of a king,
> Sans check, to good and bad: but when the planets
> In evil mixture to disorder wander,
> What plagues and what portents, what mutiny!"

This is the converse of the idea of the Ode.

The poem, like the Ode, dwells on the reign of universal law, on eternal reason, that sways alike the greater and lesser lights, the divine "pole" of the aether, the sea and all that in it is. And another poem of Cleanthes strikes the *personal* note on which the Ode ends: "Lead me, O Zeus, and thou, O Fate, whithersoever 'tis my destiny to go: thee unshrinking I will follow, and if by reason of weakness I be unwilling, follow shall I none the less." Here is the germ of:

> I call thee, I myself commend
> Unto thy guidance from this hour:
> Oh, let my weakness have an end:

which is Stoicism all over, but a Stoicism touched with the meeker spirit of a newer philosophy and a truer religion.

But we have not yet finished with the royal inconsistency of Wordsworth, which he carried to the utmost limit of lyric license. Like the Matinian bee, he levied his tribute on every kind of flower, and selected the best even from philosophies he held to be, as wholes, false. Hence we are not surprised to find a touch of Epicureanism in the midst of borrowings from Zeno: and indeed the most famous of the Epicureans was a Stoic in all but opinion. No pupil of the Porch met Fate with more dauntless courage than Lucretius, or gained a more decisive "victory" over "empty terrors" and "vain temptations." One may imagine that, when Wordsworth composed the first stanza, he was thinking of him who

> potuit rerum cognoscere causas,
> Atque metus omnes et inexorabile Fatum
> Subiecit pedibus, strepitumque Acherontis avari;

whose "quietness of thought" enabled him, amid the horrors of the dying Republic, to concentrate his mind and withdraw into himself; who won, from tumult and ceaseless change, "a repose that ever was the same." And one may regard it as all but certain that, in writing the fifth stanza,

> Stern lawgiver! yet thou dost wear
> The Godhead's most benignant grace,
> Nor know we anything so fair
> As is the smile upon thy face;
> Flowers laugh before thee on their beds,
> And fragrance in thy footing treads,

Wordsworth, consciously or subconsciously, was recalling the opening lines of the *Nature of Things*:

> Alma Venus, caeli subter labentia signa
> Quae mare navigerum, quae terras frugiferentis
> Concelebras, per te quoniam genus omne animantum
> Concipitur, visitque exortum lumina solis:
> Te, dea, te fugiunt venti, te nubila caeli
> Adventumque tuum; tibi suavis daedala tellus
> Submittit flores, tibi rident aequora ponti,
> Placatumque nitet diffuso lumine caelum.

And lastly—noting once more how widely Wordsworth spreads his net—are we too fanciful in suggesting that, in sublimating the first words of Gray's

Hymn into the first of his own, he may have had in mind the Jewish Bath-Kol, the Daughter of the Voice? We observe that the Hymn of Cleanthes speaks of the creeping things of the earth as ἰῆς μίμημα μοῦνον, but the echo of the voice divine; and as Wordsworth read that Hymn his thoughts may have strayed to that revelation which the Rabbins regarded as a substitute for the lost gift of prophecy. The "Neūm Yahweh," "Thus saith Jehovah," the direct word of God, had ceased, in later years, to be heard in Jewry, but the Bath-Kol, the echo of that Voice, still remained. It was the Bath-Kol which declared the aged Hillel to be worthy to receive the divine majesty; and it was probably a Bath-Kol which, with more terrible meaning, cried before the destruction of Jerusalem, "Arise, let us go hence," and thus revealed that God was forsaking His Temple. It may have been this, in the view of the early Christians, that proclaimed Christ, at the Baptism, the Son of God; and—though some commentators deny it—it is hard to believe that to the Jews who heard the "Phōnē" from heaven, "I have glorified my name, and again will glorify it," the voice did not sound like the same that had glorified Hillel. The mysterious "Daimonion" of Socrates, though possibly only an inward monitor, is repeatedly called by Plato a "Phōnē" or Voice; and, though Socrates tells us that it spoke to him only as a warning *against* actions that might be bad, and never as a guide to the good, it yet seems to correspond in many respects to what we call conscience, and would appear to Wordsworth as a symbol of Duty. It was, in fact, the Greek negative supplementing the positive Jewish Bath-Kol: and as such Wordsworth presents it to us here. It was not his business to assure himself by research how far the two were really identical: for his metaphorical purpose a mere hint was sufficient; and—though to him a metaphor had more objective reality than to most poets—he was no more bound to seek philosophical accuracy than Tennyson, in *In Memoriam*, was bound to give authority for his scientific statements, or to lay down with the precision of a Church council the exact sense in which Immortal Love is the Son of God. Similarly, when Wordsworth calls Duty the Daughter of the Divine Voice, he was under no obligation to define whether he means such a Bath-Kol as we may imagine to have spoken to Manoah at Zorah and to Hagar in the desert, or whether he means that echo of the Voice which God has put within us to be heard by the inward ear—stern, categorical, uncompromising, a monitor against evil and a director towards good. Nor are there many who have followed that guidance more steadily, or listened to that voice more eagerly, than the author of the *Ode to Duty*.

X

MACAULAY was a man of immense attainments, and gifted with a memory the like of which has rarely been seen. For parallels to it, indeed, we have to seek rather among men who have no books than among those to whom books are daily companions. A score of instances, illustrating his portentous powers in this respect, are given in Trevelyan's *Life*, and many others are known through tradition. Thus, for example, Dr Butler, the late Master of Trinity College, Cambridge, was fond of telling of a feat which he himself witnessed. In 1857 Macaulay came up to Cambridge after a long absence, and there met Denman, afterwards the famous judge, who had taken his fellowship at Trinity in 1843. At the fellowship examination Denman had done a remarkably good "copy" of Greek verses, which had been shown to Macaulay, and which he had glanced through—just once. On being introduced to Denman, he straightway recalled the verses, and —after characteristically touching his forehead to jog his memory—repeated them from beginning to end, to the amazement of the author himself, who had forgotten, not only the verses, but even that he had ever written them. It is probable, indeed, that, with the exception of Joseph Scaliger, who learnt

Homer in three weeks, no bookish man has had a better memory than Macaulay[1].

With such a natural capacity, Macaulay was not likely to forget the book which his father and mother, devout evangelicals of the Clapham Sect, had taught him to read in his earliest childhood. His *Life*, and, as we shall see, his writings, are full of proofs that he knew the English Bible as he knew *Paradise Lost*, the *Pilgrim's Progress*, and even the eight volumes of *Clarissa*, practically from end to end. When he wished to learn a new language, he always began with the Bible, and thus picked up the main part of the vocabulary and accidence without needing to open a lexicon. It was in this way, he tells us, that he learnt Spanish, Portuguese ("enough to read Camoens with care"), and German; and once, finding himself without other occupation, he amused himself by making out a Lapponian New Testament with the aid of a Norwegian dictionary.

He does not, it is true, appear to have troubled himself with the original Greek and Hebrew. Hebrew was one of the few dominant languages of which he knew nothing; and a casual remark in his

---

[1] There is a well-authenticated tradition of a Fellow of Wadham College, Oxford, named Hyman, who always tore up a book as soon as he had once read it, and whose shelves were filled simply with bindings. "Why keep a book when you can repeat it?" he used to say. He certainly always lectured "without book." Among the illiterate, of course, such memories are not uncommon. Mr J. C. Lawson tells us how he met in the Morea a peasant who repeated to him some thirty thousand lines, and was ready to recite more if desired.

History, dealing with the case of Thomas Aiken-
head[1], shows that he not only did not realise what
had been done in "Higher Criticism" by his time,
but despised it. Curiously enough, also, he shows
no sign of having studied the Greek Testament with
any care; indeed, I recall but one mention of that
book in the whole of his writings; and this is the
more remarkable in a man who always preferred
originals to translations in the case of the most
ordinary and unliterary secular works. But of the
English of the Authorised Version he was, as might
be expected, an intense admirer. When Lady Hol-
land, in her usual slapdash style, was talking about
the word *talented* (that bugbear of our great-grand-
fathers), and plainly showed she had never heard of
the Parable of the Talents, "I did not tell her," says
Macaulay, "though I might have done so, that a
person who professes to be a critic of the delicacies
of the English language ought to have the Bible at
his fingers' ends"—and he certainly obeyed his own
precept. Whenever—which is often—he finds an
opportunity of praising the style of Bunyan, he
seizes his chance of eulogising Bunyan's sole literary
model, "our noble translation of the Scriptures."
With the possible exception of Ruskin, whose early
upbringing was in this respect similar to his, Macaulay
is, of all the great English writers of the nineteenth
century, the one whose pages show the closest ac-

[1] *History*, chap. XXII. 1697.

quaintance with our Bible. Strong as his memory was, he refreshed it from time to time. "Sitting under" a bad preacher, on one occasion, he "withdrew his attention, and read the Epistle to the Romans."

It would obviously be impossible, in a short paper like the present, to mention even a tithe of the biblical quotations and references which stud his works. I must content myself with indicating but a few, and leave to the reader the pleasing task of noting others for himself. Suffice it to say that it will be hard to find ten or a dozen consecutive pages of Macaulay's writings, whatever the theme on which he happens to be touching, in which such allusions are entirely absent: and how much of his proverbial liveliness and vigour of style are due to this habit can be fully appraised by those only who have carefully noted such passages. Some of this liveliness, alas, is lost to the present generation. Apart from a few Lady Hollands, Macaulay could trust the readers of his own day to catch the slightest scriptural turn of phrase; for the Bible was then read and known by almost all middle-class families. Nowadays, unfortunately for literature, the state of affairs is very different; a reference to the daughters of the horse-leech or to Nadab and Abihu is no longer instantaneously appreciated. Among the minor evils of the growing ignorance of Scripture, not the least is this—that many of our greatest writers are slowly losing their force, and that many passages of Milton,

Dryden, Fuller, Lamb, and scores of others, are as flat tò present-day readers as topical jests of Aristophanes whose point has been forgotten. Ere long it will be necessary to add a note with a reference to "Proverbs xiii. 12" to explain what Macaulay meant when he said that Johnson's temper had been tried by that deferred hope which makes the heart sick; and every teacher knows that, if anything can make a passage dull, it is an annotation. When Macaulay, discussing one of Southey's most foolish and prejudiced utterances, remarked, "Here is wisdom," he could be sure that his contemporaries would at once recognise that he was quoting from the Book of Revelation; how many would recognise it now? Nor is it any adequate substitute for this instantaneous recognition to *learn* the reference and laboriously look it up; the whole zest is in the spontaneity alike of author and of reader.

The multitude of these allusions, many of which occur in this natural and half-unconscious fashion, like the overflowing quotations from Shakespeare which crowd the pages of Hazlitt[1], is the more noteworthy as it is well known how chary Macaulay was of revealing his more intimate feelings. He was a thorough Englishman in his reserve; and his early experiences had left him with more than an ordinary Englishman's horror of what is so often unjustly

[1] But more exact: for Hazlitt's memory, though capacious, was far from accurate.

called the Puritan habit of wearing one's heart upon
one's sleeve. "After the most straitest sect of our religion," he said in after-years, "I was bred a Pharisee";
and in consequence of his "Pharisaic" upbringing he
became almost extravagantly shy in the expression
of his religious feelings. At the Leeds election he
refused point-blank to answer questions as to his
religious views; and a similar reticence later lost him
his seat at Edinburgh. As Trevelyan says, even in
the company of his closest friends he scarcely ever
lifted the veil which habitually shrouded his inner-
most feelings. Thus it was only in early life that he
composed such an epitaph as that upon Henry
Martyn, or such a poem as that entitled *A Sermon
in a Churchyard*; and these did not appear till
after his death. His *Dies Irae* is a translation, and
his *Marriage of Tirzah and Ahirad* is biblical only
on the surface; yet he produced nothing even of
their kind after he had reached the age of twenty-
seven. In his later works he shows, it is true, a keen
interest in theological disputes and in ecclesiastical
history; but his knowledge and love of the Bible are
put almost exclusively at the service of literary ornament, and we trace it chiefly in subtle suggestions,
in short phrases, in stylistic tints and tones; occasionally, perhaps, in a certain moral elevation which
informs his writing with a seriousness, and even
with a grandeur, not often visible in it. But the same
sensibility which made him shun the pathetic, lest

he himself might be overcome by the sadness of the scene he described, compelled him also to a silence on religious themes which has led many superficial readers to doubt the existence in him of any religious feeling at all. He could give us the phrases of saints, but—to adopt the words which he so often quoted— while he could don their clothes he could not wear their garb.

We must look, then, in Macaulay, as his books reveal him, for a literary use of the Bible, and for no other. He betrays, it is true, his admiration of the people to whom we owe it, when, in his speech on "The Removal of Jewish Disabilities," he says, "Let us not presume to say there is no genius among the countrymen of Isaiah, no heroism among the descendants of the Maccabees." But he employs their words merely to point a sentence or round off a paragraph. Even so, however, there is much to engage our interest. Thus, for instance, when one of his young relatives, "in the true spirit of Clapham," asked whether a certain minister had received a testimonial, "I am glad, my boy," said Macaulay, "that you would not muzzle the ox that treadeth out the corn." Again, when he wished to convey in epigrammatic fashion his opinion of the shallow omniscience of Lord Brougham, he called Brougham "a sort of *semi*-Solomon, *half*-knowing everything, from the cedar to the hyssop." When the voters of Oxford University, exasperated with Peel over

Catholic Emancipation, rejected him in favour of Sir Robert Inglis, Macaulay's comment was:

> Out spake all the Pharisees
> Of the famous Oxford School,
> Not this man, but Sir Robert—
> Now Sir Robert was a fool.

Even in his childhood the same tendency was visible. When the maid took away the stones he had set up to mark the bounds of his little garden, he cried, "Cursed be Sally; for it is written, Cursed be he that removeth his neighbour's landmark"; and when more mature he kept up the practice. Of Southey's political and theological rancour he says, in the *Essay on the Colloquies,* "I do well to be angry" seems to be the dominant feeling in his mind; and he detects the same Jonah-like quality in Junius. "Doest thou well to be angry?" was the question asked in old time of the Hebrew prophet. And he answered, "I do well." Such, says Macaulay, was evidently the temper of the man who wrote the famous letters.

In describing the state of profligacy into which the nation fell after the ruin of the Commonwealth, Macaulay aptly recalls the demoniac of the New Testament.

> The Puritans boasted that the unclean spirit was cast out. The house was empty, swept, and garnished; and for a time the expelled tenant wandered through dry places, seeking rest and finding none. But the force of the exorcism was

spent. The fiend returned to his abode, and returned not alone. He took to him seven other spirits more wicked than himself, and the second possession was worse than the first.

Again, when he has to contend with those who censure the men of the Great Rebellion because of the evils which it unavoidably brought in its train —"Fifth-monarchy men, shouting for King Jesus; agitators lecturing, from the tops of tubs, on the fate of Agag; Quakers riding naked through the market-place"—he replies in the words (which perhaps he did not rightly understand) of the Three Children of Nebuchadnezzar: "Be it so. We are not careful to answer in this matter [1]"; and within three lines he has leapt from the Book of Daniel to the New Testament: "These evils were the price of our liberty. Has the acquisition been worth a sacrifice? *It is the nature of the Devil of Tyranny to tear and rend the body which he leaves.*" When he has to describe the melancholy of Dante, he compares that intense and saturnine spirit to the Sheol of Job, "a land of darkness, as darkness itself, and where the light is as darkness." Driven, by his intense hatred of Barère and by his disgust with Barère's apologists, beyond the wide limits of his ordinary vocabulary, he has recourse to that of St Paul: "Whatsoever things are false, whatsoever things are dishonest,

---

[1] *I.e.* probably "We are not particularly anxious to answer so awkward a question." Macaulay seems to mean, "The question is really one not worth answering." The R.V. has, "We have no need."

whatsoever things are unjust, whatsoever things are impure, whatsoever things are hateful, if there be any vice, and if there be any infamy, all these things were blended in Barère": a passage in which, perhaps, the extreme elaboration of the parody borders on pedantry, and which may help to explain why, as is well known, Macaulay himself did not like the essay, and refused to republish it.

It is natural enough that in dealing with a semireligious topic, such as the Dissenters' Chapels Bill, Macaulay should quote a text like "Do to others as you would that they should do unto you"; nor does the quotation show very deep biblical knowledge; but there are scores of others, turning up in all sorts of unexpected places, which *do* reveal an acquaintance, more than ordinarily wide and exact, with Holy Writ. In the essay on James Mill—not a very promising context—we light on a reference to the Pentateuch: "We are sick, it seems, like the children of Israel, of the objects of our old and legitimate worship. We pine for a new idolatry. All that is costly and all that is ornamental in our intellectual treasures must be delivered up and cast into the furnace—and there comes out this calf!" Here the sarcasm gains immensely by the retention, word for word, of the deliberately ludicrous original. There does not seem much chance of a biblical allusion in an essay on Mirabeau; but, having occasion to speak of the comparative quiet of our own revolution of 1832,

Macaulay says, "Every man went forth to his work and to his labour till the evening." Still more surprising is it to find such an allusion adorning the controversy with Michael Sadler. Sadler had made the mistake, so often made by pious men, of trying to strengthen his case by linking it with that of Christianity. "Like the Israelites," says Macaulay, "he has presumptuously and without warrant brought down the ark of God into the camp as a means of ensuring victory—and the consequence of this profanation is that, when the battle is lost, the ark is taken."

Trevelyan tells us that Macaulay, in speaking to the House of Commons, often professed to be *reminding* his auditors of facts and dates when he was really *informing* them; and this may have been done in perfect good faith, for it is certain that he greatly exaggerated the knowledge of the ordinary man. At any rate, he did not refrain, in that most secular of assemblies, from the frequent use of biblical quotations. It is well known that, when horribly bored by a man who could talk of nothing but the Beast in Revelation, he put him off by proving that the House of Commons was the Beast. It may have been this apocalyptic origin that led him to treat the House to so many scriptural allusions; it is certain at least that very few of his speeches are without them. Speaking of the dangers of anarchy, "We have all read," says he, "in our Book of Judges the fable of Jotham[1]"; but it is noteworthy that he is careful to repeat it. On so unpromising a motive as this, "That the Tower Hamlets form part of Schedule C," after "reminding" the committee of the Caesars, of Oropesa, of Squillaci, of Burke, of Aristotle—imagine such allusions in a speech of Mr Baldwin or of Mr Lloyd George!—he points his peroration with words from the New Testament; in replying to Cobbett and others on the question of Jewish disabilities, he tells his opponents that they "halt between two opinions"; on the tests in Scottish Universities, he remarks that the poor of the Free Kirk "contributed with the spirit of her who put her two mites into the treasury of Jerusalem"; speaking of the sensation caused by the Duke of Wellington's ill-timed outburst against any and every reform, he tells his hearers that "men's hearts failed them for fear."

It was perhaps not surprising that, in addressing a Scottish middle-class audience on the occasion of his re-election to Parliament in 1852, he should have relied on the biblical knowledge of his hearers. Recalling the "year of revolutions," 1848, and pointing out that England alone had come through that time unscathed, he asked, "And why is this? Why has our country, with all the ten plagues raging round

---

[1] The same fable recurred to his mind when, in 1852, Lord John Russell offered him a place in the Cabinet. "Let them go to the bramble," he said.

her, been a land of Goshen? Everywhere else was
the thunder and the lightning running along the
ground—a very grievous storm—a storm such as
there was none like it since man was on the earth;
yet everything tranquil here; and then again thick
night, darkness that might be felt; and yet light in
all our dwellings." Nor was it surprising that he
should expect Edinburgh men to catch the allusion
when he said that the "flood of barbaric invasion
would no more return to cover the earth." Scotland,
then, even more than now, knew its Bible. But
Macaulay gave the squires and manufacturers of the
Palmerstonian House of Commons fully as rich
measure of biblical quotation as he gave his North
British constituents.

In the 1844 speech on the State of Ireland he told
his hearers that the Irish Catholic had been "a
mere Gibeonite, a hewer of wood and a drawer of
water"; ten minutes later he added that the country
had "suffered many things of many physicians," not
the least inefficient of the practitioners being Sir
Robert Peel himself. Speaking in 1845 on the Corn
Laws, he bids Members "begin with the Book of
Genesis, and come down to the Parliamentary De-
bates"; and he helps them over part of the way by
referring to the account of Pharaoh's dream: "The
thin ears had blighted the full ears; the lean kine had
devoured the fat kine; the days of plenty were over."
It is certain that Macaulay's audiences must, in the

course of years, have been reminded, or informed, of many scores of incidents or passages in sacred literature. No other Parliamentary orator, in all probability, since the days of Prynne and Barebone, can have woven into the thread of his discourses so many scriptural phrases. Even John Bright is not so rich in biblical allusion as Macaulay.

In the *Essay on History*, Macaulay passes a just censure on the Roman neglect of Hebrew literature —a censure that the present age, which shows the same neglect with less excuse, might well take to heart.

The sacred books of the Hebrews, books which, considered merely as human compositions, are invaluable to the critic, the antiquarian, and the philosopher, seem to have been utterly unnoticed by them. The peculiarities of Judaism, and the rapid growth of Christianity, attracted their notice. They made war against the Jews. They made laws against the Christians. But they never opened the books of Moses. Juvenal quotes the Pentateuch with censure (*Sat. XIV.* 102). The author of the treatise on the Sublime quotes it with praise (*Longinus*, IX. 9); but both of them quote it errone-ously. When we consider what sublime poetry, what curious history, what striking and peculiar views of the divine nature and of the social duties of men, are to be found in the Jewish Scriptures, when we consider that two sects on which the attention of the Government was constantly fixed appealed to those Scriptures as the rule of their faith and practice, this indifference is astonishing. The fact seems to be that the Greeks admired only themselves, and that the Romans admired only themselves and the Greeks.

And he proceeds to dwell on the narrowness and

sameness of thought that were the result of this indifference. From *this* narrowness, at any rate, Macaulay himself was free.

But it was, as we have hinted, more in slight touches and subtle allusions that his knowledge of Scripture is best shown; and it is in watching for such half-quotations, "glimmering," in Thackeray's phrase, "below the surface of the narrative," that the reader will find his keenest interest. "The *Marah* of Byron's misanthropy is never dry"; "one who had swallowed the Scotch Declaration would scarcely strain at the Covenant"; the effigy of Chatham, "graven by a cunning hand"; "no man more readily held up the left cheek to those who had smitten the right"; "there was another sowing of the wind and another reaping of the whirlwind"; "portioning out all those wealthy regions from Dan to Beersheba"; "no oath inspires the confidence which is produced by the *yea, yea,* and *nay, nay,* of a British envoy"; "what Bute already possessed was vanity and vexation of spirit"; "the iron had not yet entered into his soul[1]";—such are a few examples, culled almost at random, which show how the phraseology of our translation of the Bible had become part and parcel of Macaulay's mind. "If the tree which Socrates planted and Plato watered is to be judged of by its flowers and leaves, it is the noblest of trees"; here,

---

[1] This is the Prayer Book version, Ps. cv. 18. The right translation is almost certainly that of the A.V. margin.

in the essay on Bacon, are two sayings, one of Christ and one of Paul, blended into a single whole. On statesmen like Theramenes and Talleyrand, we are told in the essay on Temple, rests the curse of Reuben: "Unstable as water, thou shalt not excel." In two passages, dealing with the sham piety which Madame de Maintenon introduced into the Court of Louis XIV, Macaulay employs the phrase, "A fashion it was, and like a fashion it passed away." Who recognises that this is a quotation from St Paul's first epistle to the Corinthians? The Presbyterians of Scotland (*History*, chap. XVI. 1690) might feel that "the second temple was not equal to the first" —here is a reference to the second chapter of Haggai; but "they felt for William a grateful affection such as the restored Jews had felt for the heathen Cyrus" —here is a reference to Ezra and the Deutero-Isaiah. "The principles of liberty were the Anathema Maranatha[1] of every fawning dean"—here the *Milton* quotes *Corinthians*; "the race accursed was again driven forth to wander (like Cain) on the face of the earth, and to be a byword and a shaking of the head to the nations"—here the *Milton* quotes (this time from the Authorised Version) the forty-fourth Psalm. Out of the abundance of the heart the mouth speaketh; and this abundance of scriptural knowledge was bound to colour Macaulay's vocabulary and phraseology.

[1] Of course, "Maranatha," "The Lord is at hand," is not really a part of the anathema.

But we have not yet said all. The debt of Macaulay to the Bible is by no means exclusively shown in his words; it appears also in his peculiar mannerism. As a stylist he owes, of course, much to his Greek and Latin studies, and to his wide knowledge of our own literature. But that short, sharp, balanced sentence of his was not, assuredly, derived from his reading of Cicero or Demosthenes, nor from the earlier masters of English prose. It differs markedly even from the antithesis of Seneca and from the epigram of Tacitus; nor is it really like the brevity and point of Bacon. Something similar, certainly, is to be seen in Johnson; and many of Macaulay's *other* characteristics are to be observed in Burke, who, like his disciple, was both a writer and an orator. But the real source of this marked and unmistakable feature—of that which to many people is *par excellence* Macaulayese—is to be sought elsewhere. It was learnt from the short, sharp "parallelism" of Hebrew poetry; from that antithetic collocation of clauses, sometimes by way of repetition, sometimes by way of correction or even contradiction, sometimes by way of extension, which lends such vigour to the retorts of Job, such vividness to the descriptions of Nahum or of Isaiah; nay, which often gives force to the sayings of our Lord Himself. A critic, indeed, who should set out to analyse Macaulay's style, will find himself unconsciously repeating the analysis which Lowth long ago gave

of the *Sacra Poesis Hebraeorum*, with its "synony-
mous" parallelism, its "antithetic," its "synthetic,"
and its "climactic." Nay, I have sometimes thought
that the double "introverted parallelism" of Macaulay's epitaph on a Jacobite:

> To my true king I offered, free from stain,
> Courage and faith, vain faith and courage vain,

may have sprung rather from such verses as Isaiah's
"Ephraim shall not envy Judah, and Judah shall not
vex Ephraim," than from some Greek *chiasmus*. Be
this as it may, the origin of Macaulay's general
manner is clear, whatever may be thought of single
passages. If anyone doubts this, let him read a page
of the *Essays* and then a chapter of the Book of
Proverbs; remembering, as he does so, that Macaulay
was brought up on such chapters, and got them by
heart in the most susceptible and formative years of
his life. "Wax to receive, and marble to retain," his
mind took from those early studies an impress which
it never lost, and which is visible in the latest words
he ever wrote[1].

When the essay on Milton first appeared, in the
Edinburgh Review of 1825, the editor, Jeffrey, said
to Macaulay, "The more I think of it, the more I

---

[1] This is literally the case. In the hasty and almost illegible fragment
which concludes the *History*, he tells how William, on the Sunday,
stamped the parchment which secured the passing of the Abjuration
Bill; "and the most rigid Pharisee could hardly deny that it was lawful
to save the State, even on the Sabbath."

wonder where on earth you picked up that style."
One source, and that far from the least important,
of the style ought to have been obvious to so widely
read a man as Jeffrey. It was the Authorised Version
of the Old and New Testaments, issued in 1611.

xi

SWINBURNE[1]

THE death of Swinburne may well arouse in us thoughts of sadness. "The cease of majesty dies not alone," and with him passes away a phase in our literature. It is true that his last really characteristic work, the glorious *Tale of Balen*, appeared as long ago as 1896, and that even the *servum pecus* of imitators and parodists is now almost silent; but while he lived the race of the giants seemed not to have utterly departed.

Action and reaction are the law of all life, and in one aspect Swinburne represents a reaction. He was born in 1837; when he came to his precocious maturity the star of Tennyson was in the ascendant, and to some extent his career was determined by a more or less conscious revulsion from the Tennysonian dominance. But he had too much of what he himself called "self-sufficience" to be the mere protagonist of a rebellion. He felt, it is true, that Tennyson, after reaching his climacteric in 1842, had been recreant to the romantic spirit which he had once so faithfully followed. Particularly did Swinburne feel this with reference to the *Idylls of the King*, with

---

[1] This was written just after Swinburne's death, and may have a documentary interest as conveying views which were pretty generally held at that time.

their Arthurian allegory of a Victorian and bourgeois perfection; and he laughs at the insular narrowness which made the hero of Mallory a mere Prince Albert, and which concluded the *Princess* with "the shrill, unmistakable accent, not of a provincial deputy, but of a provincial school-boy." Nevertheless, while he never altered this view, and while his *Tristram* and his *Balen* were doubtless largely dictated by the desire to recall the nation to a better ideal of romance than the Tennysonian, he did Tennyson full justice.

To the making of Swinburne, and to his preparation for the part he had to fill, nature and training contributed in different but equally marked degrees. He was born, if ever poet was, a lyrist and a romantic: he would have sung if he had been quite untaught, but no English poet, Milton and Gray perhaps excepted, ever brought to his task so wide and deep a culture; a culture which began with his very earliest years and continued to the end of his life. He knew a dozen languages and literatures, and he was absolute master of at least three: French, Greek, and English. He wrote French like a Frenchman, Greek like Sir Richard Jebb, and English in the way we all know. He had a memory which was the astonishment of everyone who came near him, and which retained enormous passages from all sorts of writers for any length of time. Probably no one that ever lived, even among professional scholars, knew English poetry, or at least the English drama, more widely and more accurately. But he was far from being the slave of his favourites. He disliked the "botching" of Euripides; but he learnt from Euripides, and his classic plays are more Euripidean than Sophoclean. He cared little for Byron; but he knew his Byron as even Byron's adoring contemporaries did not know him. He despised Boileau and all his school; yet even from Boileau his catholic taste gained something. He has a word of eulogy for Pope himself.

But from his earliest days there were four or five great masters who seized a sway over him that they never lost. Coleridge he never ceased to regard as the master metrist of English lyric poets. "For absolute melody and splendour it were hardly rash to call *Kubla Khan* the first poem in the language." Shelley, perhaps his true master, held in his mind "the same rank in lyric as Shakespeare in dramatic poetry: supreme and without a second of his race." The odes of Keats attained "nearly to the very utmost beauty possible to human words." As for his idolatry of Victor Hugo, is it not the burden of almost every volume he wrote? But added to all this was a more surprising enthusiasm for the classic verse and chiselled prose of Landor, a man indeed of impressive stature, but different in style and in cast of mind from his admirer. This worship of the great classicist is a type of Swinburne's whole genius, a genius primarily romantic and lyrical; but nourished, strengthened, and—we make bold to add—

restrained by a close and loving study of the classical models. But for the classics Swinburne's poetry would have been a mere chaos; as it is, its passion, its *abandon*, its frenzy has rarely strayed beyond the limits of a moderating art. As the worship of Hugo typifies that rhetoric which was the besetment of Swinburne in his uninspired moments, and which yet saves his worst work from insipidity, so his worship of Landor typifies that restraint which saved his inspiration from self-destructive overflow.

Swinburne has himself, in his essay on Keats, spoken of the power of *assimilation*—not, of course, imitation—as the sign of an original genius. That Swinburne possessed the imitative faculty scores of passages, both in his prose and in his verse, could be adduced to prove. We might point specially to the story of St Dorothy in the first series of *Poems and Ballads*. Even here, however, there is more of Swinburne than of Chaucer; for Swinburne's assimilative power was even greater than his imitative. Of this the proofs are innumerable, and we have even seen their number adduced, by critics with more learning than taste, as indications that he was only a manipulator of other men's rhythms and not a creative artist. For example, something like the lilt of "If Love were what the rose is" has been discovered in a forgotten lyric of Dryden's; another of his measures appears in rudimentary form among Waller's poems; the relation between Praed's anapaests and *Dolores* is plain for all to see. But in every case the inimitable melody lies precisely in the one differential touch that Swinburne has added. Scores of songs have the *metre* of *Rococo*; but whence came the peculiar sweetness which makes us fancy it a new and unheard-of thing? Swinburne borrows, in fact, his melodies as Milton and Virgil borrowed their Homeric similes: he makes them his own. Picking up for a penny a copy of the *Rubáiyát*—then the forgotten work of an unknown author—he saw at a glance the genius in it, went home, and produced in *Laus Veneris* a poem in the same measure, with something of the same tone, but with all the Swinburnian marks on it. But the measure is, after all, *not* the same. A single touch has converted it into a new one. The centre of gravity of FitzGerald's stanza, like that of Horace's alcaic, is the third unrhymed line. This third line is in *Laus Veneris* made to rhyme with the corresponding line of the next, and thus arises a stanza of eight lines instead of four; a new, linked, and lengthened measure which immediately assumes a character of its own, and challenges a future different from that of FitzGerald's.

The same is true of his metre generally. It is futile to deny him originality; it is more futile to suppose that his rhythms and rhymes sprang up ready made. With the prophetic ear of youth he caught a certain melody, innate in the English language—a melody which it is strange that anyone should ever have denied to it. After this melody Byron, Moore, and many others had set out in clumsy and fruitless chase; Praed had occasionally overtaken it, but had used it for lower purposes. It was, we have no doubt, in Shelley that Swinburne first saw its limitless possibilities; the lilt of *Arethusa* recurs again and again among the many waters of his verse; but that something of Coleridge also went to the making of his special music we doubt just as little. It was Coleridge who had reclaimed for English poetry the lost metrical freedom of the old ballad, and had informed this regained freedom with a beauty and a subtlety only to be attained by the most sensitive art; such a beauty, in fact, as had not been heard in shorter measures since the *Pearl*. Following him, Swinburne saw that there yet remained, in the *natural* cadences of English, a vein of melody yet unexhausted, nay, except by Shelley, almost untouched. English unforced metre *naturally* runs in trips and so-called anapaests; the *regular* succession of iambics and trochees is only attained by some degree, more or less pronounced, of violence. To this conception he added the no less important one of *quantity*, the secret of the harmony of Milton and Tennyson; not, of course, the rigid system of Sidney or Gabriel Harvey, but that *weight* which is as essential to English verse as to Latin itself. Of this mingling of quantity and accent, which never ceases to be English and yet is always Greek, a type can be found in his exquisite *Sapphics*. There we have the *spirit* of Greek quantity married to English accent; no mere lifeless transplantation of classical laws, but simply the same principles observed as would make *any* measure melodious—light syllables in the light places, and weighty in the weighty. On these principles all Swinburne's lyrics, anapaestic or iambic, were alike constructed, and thus it is that they almost invariably sing themselves. This it is that made the choruses of *Atalanta* burst on those who first heard them like a new revelation in the power of sound.

And other writers were not slow to borrow from him the melodies he had opened to their ken. The metre of *Dolores* was taken up by a crowd of imitators, and parodied by many a rhymer. That of the *Hymn to Proserpine* has had a better fate. Appropriated by an original mind, and stamped with a new and vigorous character, it became the metre of Dr Arthur Way's noble *Odyssey*. As for the songs in *Atalanta*, do we not know that one of them provided the stanza for no less famous a poem than Bret Harte's *Heathen Chinee*? Could any proof be clearer that the rhythms of Swinburne have become part and parcel of our poetical possessions?

"Rhyme," says Swinburne himself, "is the native condition of lyric verse in English; a rhymeless lyric is a maimed thing, and halts and stammers in the delivery of its message." Rightly then, though he could write blank verse with the best, did he weave into his lyric poems the most wonderful winding webs of rhyme; not scorning the refrain, nor, it is needless to add, neglecting the consonantal rhyme of alliteration. He probably added more new metres to English poetry than anyone since Chaucer; and, from the point of view of skill in rhyme, there has assuredly never been his equal. For an approach to a parallel to the two hundred and sixty nine-lined stanzas of *Balen*, each stanza with but three rhymes, we must go back to the hundred linked stanzas of the *Pearl*. It is true that he refused to tie himself to rigid exactness. We find plenty of "rich rhymes"; we find in *Balen* the noun *pass* rhyming in Chaucerian fashion with the same word used as a verb; we have *hiss* rhymed with *his*, *ours* with *hours*; nay, in multitudes of cases the very same word does duty twice over. The much-enduring word *was* has to rhyme with *pass* oftener than we care to count; and, on the multitudinous occasions he has to use the word *love*, he must have been glad that no scruples hindered him from compelling *of* and *enough*, as well as *move* and *grove*, to rhyme with it. After this we are not surprised that, in the wonderful *tour de force Faustine*, the rhyme, required no less than forty times, is helped out by pressing *sin*, *wherein*, and the like into the service. Nor would his relationship to the clan of Rossetti be completely manifest unless he had given us in full measure the peculiar rhyme

of which Keats in *Endymion* set the fashion, and
which was so well ridiculed by Bayard Taylor, but
to which, as Swinburne uses it, we confess an
attachment:

> The hard sun, as thy petals knew,
>> Covered the heavy moss-*water*;
> Thou wert not worth green *midsummer*,
>> Nor fit to live to August blue,
> O sundew, not remembering her.

With this mastery of rhyme, with this royal despotism over the resources of the language, he remains
(Milton apart) the greatest master of sound, pure
and simple, in English; a reed, in Tennyson's words,
through which melody was naturally blown. With
all this technical equipment, it remains to be seen
what was his "message": and here at once we light
on the region of controversy. It is common to say
of him that he could not think, that his sound is a
mere echo of nothing. Swinburne himself has in-
directly dealt with this charge. "It is said sometimes
that a man may have a strong and perfect style who
has nothing to convey worth conveyance under
cover of it"; and at this point, in our copy of the
book, some echoer of the common criticism has
pencilled the comment: "Thou art the man." But
Swinburne proceeds: "This is a favourite saying of
men who have no words in which to convey the
thoughts they have not. But it remains for them to
prove as well as assert that beauty and power of

expression can accord with emptiness or sterility of matter." This we believe to be essentially a fair reply. Words that burn *must* imply the thoughts that breathe. And in Swinburne's case the thoughts are there. They are not, it is true, the penetrating thoughts of a Goethe, nor do we recognise in them that strange insight which is the mark of Shakespeare. But he shows thought as lyric poetry understands the word; intangible and impalpable, not easily to be packed into the narrowness of prose, but none the less real and reproductive. It is a shallow criticism which confuses the ethereal with the empty. It must be admitted that, in his verse as in his prose, he often struggles long before he arrives at the consummation he desires; like Spenser, he requires room in which to move; but he almost invariably (to use a convenient slang phrase of our day) "gets there" at last. And when the garrulity is so musical as his, it may well be pardoned. Many a poem of his may be too long to be unstintedly praised; it is not too long for every verse to be loved. He has not, of course, the condensation of Milton, which longs to wring from every word the fullest meaning, charged with all its associations, that the word can bear; nor could he, like Rossetti, prune down whole volumes into single poems. And yet how few, after all, are the lines that we would willingly miss, even in the longest poems!

Of inspiring themes he had plenty; but—and here

we reach the secret of the charge of deficiency in material—they were too general, too remote, and too subjective to appeal to the many. For example, though he was a true patriot, he was too cosmo-politan to appeal to the English mind as the some-what insular patriotism of Tennyson so easily did. He loved France too well to have ever flung out cheap sneers at "the red fool-fury of the Seine," and he lost many an English admirer in consequence. He loved liberty; but he was as enthusiastic for the liberty of Italy, Hungary, or Russia as he was for the liberty of England. A single verse on some Hampden or Cromwell would have done more for him than all his impassioned poems on Mazzini—a hero as great as either, but not an Englishman. He hated tyranny, and denounced it as the Hebrew prophets denounced the Assyrian tyrants; but the men he denounced were Napoleon III, Caesar, or the Czar, whose despotism did not particularly con-cern Englishmen. Again, he had the true romantic spirit; as we have seen, it was impossible to him to moralise the story of King Arthur. He would have been as incapable as William Morris himself of turn-ing *Tristram* or *Balen* into a disguised sermon. Hence that kind of appeal which Tennyson could make to his countrymen by such a poem as *Guinevere* was quite impossible to Swinburne. He might have written *The Lady of Shalott*; he would certainly never have tried to write an *Elaine*. He had, as we shall see, no objection to teaching in poetry; he thought with the Greeks that art must justify itself as being useful; but he thought with the Greeks also that the teaching must come naturally, and must in every case be subordinate to the main object of poetry, which is simply to be beautiful. Hence he objected, with Landor, to certain parts of the *Divine Comedy*, not because they are theological, but because they are grotesque or even ugly; and he preferred the *Prelude* to the *Excursion* not because the latter has more philosophy in it than the former, but because the philosophy is unpoetical. On the other hand, the total absence of tangible content did not hinder him from assigning to *Kubla Khan* a place in the very front rank. It was divinely beautiful, and that was enough. The same canons apply to his own work. The *Hymn to Proserpine* is immortal, not because its teaching is true, but because its expression is beautiful. The "poems" on the Boer War are condemned, not because they deal with politics, but because they lack the spirit that quickeneth.

Religion, again, was ruled out from his available sources of inspiration and influence, and that too although he was perhaps less pagan than is generally thought. He was an intense admirer of the religious poems of Christina Rossetti, and regarded "Passing away, saith the world, passing away" as the highest achievement in the difficult sphere of purely Christian poetry. Nor was he deterred from admiring the

Atheist's Tragedy by the somewhat ferocious and unsparing manner in which Tourneur depicts the crimes of his atheist. But he was certainly Hellene; he was perhaps less religious than any other great English poet. He had many admirations, but only one worship, that of beauty; and this is a poor exchange for the faith and morals which Milton held. It is no complaint against a poet that he does not directly preach religion; but the poet in whom we can discern no undercurrent of religious feeling misses the surest way to touch the universal heart. He could sing with unmatched pathos a dirge over the old faiths; he could sing a kind of Pantheism in *Hertha*; but in both cases the real faith that he sang was different from the ostensible one; his real goddess was the same beauty which he saw equally in romance because it dealt with a transfigured past, and in the Greek belief because it was dead. Still further, much as he loved the *Ode to Duty*, he could not with Wordsworth hymn the divine in nature, because he was far from sure whether nature was divine. Nor could he, like Goethe in *Das Göttliche*, have risen from the contemplation of the moral in man to a belief in the existence of higher beings, moral also, and mighty helpers in the great war between good and evil. In spite of his love of the general, he never seems to have attained either to the conception of good as a single entity, to be adored as such, or to the Christian conception of good as expressed in a Person. In this respect his utmost faith is represented by his recurring phrase: "Whatever gods there be." Few poets, as we shall see, have had a clearer vision of certain *aspects* of the good; few indeed have been more indifferent to the good in itself.

Equally conspicuous in its absence is a belief in immortality, an absence which may well have accounted for his want of interest in ethic as a spiritual principle. And Swinburne, in this respect, went beyond mere agnosticism; he becomes dogmatic in his denial, and even elevates annihilation into a kind of creed, from which some comfort is to be derived. Death, to him, was the end of all, the gift of Proserpina was eternal and unchanging. As he says in that verse which has of late been quoted perhaps oftener than any other: "No life lives for ever, and dead men rise up never"; we have to be content, nay, we have to triumph, in our "sleep eternal in an eternal night." He has none of the sad misgiving of a William Watson at the prospect; none of the awe at "the apparition, the veiled sign, the beckoning finger bidding him forgo" the fellowship and converse of this world. Secure of the short immortality that fame gives, he welcomed the annihilation which in his belief death must offer him.

Nor, again, can we trace in him, to any profound degree, that peculiar vein of symbolism which fills the thoughts of Maeterlinck, of Hauptmann, and, among ourselves, of Mr Yeats, "Æ.," and others who are expressing now in lovely language the inner soul of things. That the invisible is the truly real, that the material, apart from the spiritual, is an inexplicable contradiction, he was of course conscious; but the consciousness did not, as with the poets we have named, underlie every word he wrote, and form the background of all his ideas. To us, indeed, his genius seems to have been, after all, essentially concrete, and to have kept at least one foot always on the solid earth: and this to us accounts for the sensuousness of much in his most ethereal poetry—a sensuousness which has, indeed, been unduly criticised, but which certainly marks a limitation in his poetic outlook. It is this which forms the true distinction between him and his master Shelley. We do not forget the many poems in which he enters the outer court of such a mysticism; but we do not believe that he ever penetrates into the inner shrine.

At the same time, a certain love of generality, of wide views and immense conceptions, while to be carefully distinguished from mysticism on the one hand and from vagueness on the other, robbed him of many a reader. After his early lyrics of personal passion he came, as is well known, to prefer the Ode, whose very essence is the expression of the feelings of a multitude, of a nation, of a whole species, as contrasted with those individual emotions which a Heine loves to voice. The personality of the vast, this was a conception never absent from his mind at one period of his career. Hence many readers, who saw their own feelings, so to speak, absorbed in the great average, were repelled by him.

But if all this be admitted—and we might add to our list—what a variety of fields of poetry did he not touch! What a multitude of themes did he not find to yield him a marvellous inspiration! Love of liberty and hatred of tyranny, an intense feeling for nationality, the past with its romance, the future with its hopes, the achievements of great and good men, the crimes of bad men—all these furnished him with inexhaustible themes for passionate eulogy or for killing denunciation. Never, in truth, was there a man with a higher power of admiring: wherever he saw excellence of any kind he praised it in almost unmeasured language. He was carried away by the splendour of a genius like Victor Hugo's or of a nobility like Mazzini's, and sighed for more superlatives than the English speech affords, in order to express his limitless admiration.

He had also an equally unbounded hatred of cruelty and oppression in all its forms, and a vigour in denouncing them never excelled. All his rhetorical force came to the aid of his poetical genius when he started to scarify the Czar, or to hold up to ever-lasting infamy the murders by which Napoleon the Little made his way to his uneasy throne. And all this is raised almost to the height of prophecy by its union with a sense of the inevitable and universal power of Right. For apparent success, divorced from goodness, he has all the lofty scorn of an Epictetus; and dull indeed must be those who are not stung into some enthusiasm by his splendid indignation and by his magnificent eulogies of virtue, however lowly. We may apply to him surely much of the praise which he himself gave to Morris:

> No braver, no trustier, no purer,
>   No stronger and clearer a soul,
> Bore witness more splendid and surer
>   For manhood made perfect and whole,
> Since man was a warrior and dreamer,
>   Than his who in hatred of wrong
> Would fain have risen a redeemer
>   By sword or by song.

It is this spirit which lends reality to that somewhat dreary series of poems that filled the interval between *Erechtheus* and *Tristram*, and the longer one between *Tristram* and *Balen*. Many of these are empty of everything but splendour of sound, but here and there we light on passages or whole poems that are alive with this nobility of feeling. Even where the *poetical* inspiration is absent, *this* inspiration is often visible. Especially, perhaps, is this the case with the plays, and not least with the great trilogy of Mary Stuart. The charm of *Marino Faliero* lies mainly in its superb and astonishing rhetoric; *Locrine* and *Rosamund, Queen of the Lombards*, in spite of the

extreme repression of the verse, are essentially
romances cast into a dramatic form; the tragedy of
The Sisters, while indeed fine, is pitched in a low
key; but *Mary Stuart* is one exact transcript from
history, in which, while the facts alone speak, they
are allowed to speak with absolute faithfulness their
condemnation of passion and crime. We did not
need Swinburne's essay on Mary to inform us that
in these plays he had done but the smallest violence
to fact, and none at all to what he conceived to be
the Queen's actual character: and the judgment of
fate upon her deeds is accurately echoed in the dramas.
Chastelard is the tragedy of a young man ruined by
love for a beautiful and dominating, but essentially
non-moral, woman; one to whom the true heights
of pure love are unknown, but capable of the utmost
extremes of passion and ambition. *Bothwell* shows
us the fortunes of that same commanding woman
when she, as was inevitable, falls in turn a prey to
a passion for a man more reckless even than herself;
and in *Mary Stuart* we see the long-drawn vengeance
working itself out, and the story carried through
to its foregone and fated conclusion: the death of
Chastelard cries for death in turn, and is satiated at
last. The moral, though never obtruded, is as plain
to read as that of Shakespeare's *Macbeth*; and, that
none may miss it, it is pointed by the motto from
the *Choephoroe*: "In return for murderous stroke a
murderous stroke be given; let him that doeth suffer;

so hath been the law from the beginning of the world." Here, if anywhere, those who deny restraint, ethical feeling, or intellectual power to Swinburne, must often find themselves strangely at fault. Retributive justice has rarely been more plainly preached since Aeschylus. The patient watching of Mary Beaton, through all that "long, sad score of years" since the death of Chastelard; her ceaseless resolve, "through all these chances, never to leave her till she die"; and her final bitter satisfaction, are surely among the deepest, truest and most *moral* things in all dramatic poetry.

But the three great motives which inspire Swinburne's poetry, whenever it is really such, are: love, mankind as a whole, and the sea.

As a love-poet the position of Swinburne is unique. No other has apparently described all the emotions of a lover so fully, or even so realistically, as he; and yet we are forbidden to regard his most realistic descriptions as photographs of his own life. We have his own statement that they are *studies* of passion and sensation, "neither confessions of positive fact nor excursions of absolute fancy." Indeed, it is impossible that any one man can have actually passed through *all* the experiences hinted at in these poems; he has obviously projected himself, in certain cases, as far out of himself as Browning in *Men and Women*. On the other hand, they are *genuine* studies; they are not mere literary imitations of a

French *genre*. *Laus Veneris*, for example, perhaps the most strongly censured of them all, is on the one hand a dramatic monologue based on an imagined situation, and on the other a hymn of passion fully realised and set on fire by the appropriating power of the poet. Thus these poems differ from those of Goethe, Heine, and others in being more impersonal; and yet the study is so exact, the poet makes himself so one with the subject described, that even the love-poems of Goethe and Heine, nay, those of Burns himself, appear less actual. The delusion is due to that concreteness in Swinburne's genius on which we have already touched.

Strange to say, it is precisely these love-poems, so strongly censured for their realism, that have been fixed upon by one of Swinburne's keenest critics to prove the thesis that he never expressed emotions of his own, but always, like a professional letter-writer, those appropriate to someone else; and this, says the critic in question, proves his inferiority to Burns. But this judgment needs to be very carefully qualified. The poems are *sincere*; they are felt to the inmost depths of the poet's being. But if the critic means that their sincerity is *poetical* sincerity only, he is probably right. They are passions artistically remembered, as an old man remembers with advantages the deeds he did at Agincourt. It would be foolish to deny that he ever was at Agincourt: it would be equally foolish to believe that he had been quite so heroic as he makes out. Throughout all these poems, as another excellent critic has observed, emotion always preponderates over sensation, and the idea often over the emotion. They are studies of moods, intellectually analysed but imaginatively pictured; and the same hand that has drawn the delirium of love has also, with equal power, drawn the weariness of satiety, the pang of separation, the agony of remorse. We can no more take literally these poems than those others in which the longing for death—a longing cheerfully endured for forty years—is thrown into imperishable words.

The second great motive, a feeling for mankind as a whole, played the main part in Swinburne's poetry during the interval between the appearance of *Poems and Ballads* and the return to Greece in *Erechtheus*. No poet can afford to be too definite; but on the other hand, if he has no definite idea before his mind he runs the risk of losing himself in mere vacuity. The solid substratum of Swinburne's poetry of humanity was found primarily in Italy and secondarily in France. And as France tended to dwindle in his mind into Victor Hugo, so Italy tended to concentrate, nay, to dilate, itself into the noble, colossal, but perfectly balanced figure of Mazzini. The crimes of Napoleon III were to Swinburne largely summed up in the banishment of the great poet; and Swinburne's denunciations of the

Second Empire were often but a rendering into English of the terrible *Châtiments* of Hugo. In Mazzini, similarly, Swinburne saw the incarnation of what he regarded as best in the man of politics; and this it was that gave definiteness, edge, and body to ideas which might otherwise have faded into cloud. Swinburne's poetry, in fact, like Italy itself, was saved from anarchy by Mazzini: and this too while, with a true instinct, he kept to the poet's part of inspiring others, and left details to the men of action. Thus the Italian poems are eulogies, well deserved it is true, rather than either essays or criticisms. It was natural, therefore, that when the crowning aim of Mazzini failed of accomplishment, Swinburne's panegyric, doubtless already embryonic in his mind, had to seek another theme on which to express itself. True liberty, as he understood it, had not been achieved: the work was maimed and imperfect. When, therefore, Italy, though freed from foreign domination, became a kingdom and not a republic, Swinburne held his hand, and reserved his triumph for the true consummation as it took place in France ten years later. His *Ode on the Proclamation of the French Republic* is the real sequel to his Italian poems. These are the works which link Swinburne with Shelley on one of his sides, as the love-lyrics link him with Shelley on another.

The final and perhaps most pervasive of all the influences that have moulded Swinburne is his passion for the sea. It would be instructive to count the number of allusions to the sea, by way of simile, metaphor, or general reference, that lie scattered throughout the whole work of Swinburne. It is certain that few English poets have felt the wonder of the sea, in all its moods, as he has done. The fury of it spoke to the Northumbrian as it spoke to the author of *Andreas* a thousand years before; its beauty and softness, visioned from his early Isle of Wight home, were clothed by his fancy in all the dreaming languor of the Idle Lake as seen by Spenser. And it was the sea *itself* that appealed to him. As Mr James Douglas has said, "Most of our poets, from Campbell to Kipling, regard the sea either as a stage for our naval heroes, or as a material for metaphor, or as a stock-pot of sentiment, or as a reservoir of rhetoric. But Swinburne did for the sea what Wordsworth did for the land. His clean rapture in the sea is free from literary affectation." This is as true as it is well expressed. What touch of falseness the keenest scent for rhetoric may discover in other of Swinburne's poems is absent here. Death was the love of his youth; Italy of his manhood; the sea he loved from his earliest days to his last: it was to his outer eye what Greece was to the eye of his mind, and it supplied to him the concrete image in which all his tempestuous ideas glassed themselves. From contact with the sea, like his own Tristram in the glorious and often-quoted passage,

his poetry gained an overflowing and irresistible
life:

> And scarcely seemed its life a part of earth,
> But the life kindled of a fiery birth
> And passion of a new-begotten son,
> Between the live sea and the living sun.

It is difficult, indeed, to part from so enthralling
a subject as this. But, after all, to analyse great
poetry is to run the risk of destroying it. Even
Swinburne's own criticism, though sometimes illuminating, was often content with simple admiration.
Poetry to him, as to Shelley, was "a power which
comes and goes like a dream, and which none can ever
trace." We shall, therefore, make no further attempt
at criticism. Still less shall we say a word in pity or
censure. We prefer to end on a note of gratitude.
"Render thanks to the Giver, England, for thy son."
Like Swinburne himself, when he wrote of the
"frayed wings" of Villon, we would rather be glad
in what he did than waste our time wondering what
he might have done. "Ave atque vale."

> For thee, O now a silent soul, our brother,
> Take at our hands this garland, and farewell.

xii

JOSEPH CONRAD

THERE is nearly as much pleasure in uttering an artless platitude as in traversing the pathless woods; and we shall therefore begin with one. Man is an imitative animal, and lazy. Above all, he likes someone else to form his opinions for him; and he will rather be wrong with the feeblest mock-Plato he can find than be right by his own efforts. Let but some prophet assume a tone of authority and utter any opinion, however groundless, and he will at once secure followers. Should the opinion chime in luckily with the tone of thought of the time, it will be welcomed, repeated, and finally held as an article of faith, the rejection of which incurs all the penalties of heresy. Some theories, totally without basis, have in this way been gradually established, until it has required almost a revolution to pull them down. Readers of Lucian will remember how, just after the self-immolation of Peregrinus, he told a boring interviewer, by way of jest, that he had seen an eagle rise up from the flames of martyrdom. Some time later, returning to the spot, he found the eagle an article of faith among the followers of the prophet, with multitudes of eye-witnesses to vouch for it.

Certain political creeds, for example, such as that of the Divine Right of Kings, or that of the Satanic

16-2

origin of the French Revolution, were of this kind. The few daring disputants who asked for proofs were either ignored or shouted down. Proof, if supplied at all—and the dogma was generally regarded as intuitively evident and all the more certain because it could not be proved—was usually of the sort that is invented to bolster up a foregone conclusion, and stood, therefore, in more need of defence than the thesis itself. In reading such demonstrations we are irresistibly reminded of the conduct of Frederick the Great with regard to Silesia. The army is on the march to occupy the province; only when the capital is taken do the statesmen and diplomats produce their laboured dissertations to show that Silesia is legally a Hohenzollern appanage.

But the same thing is to be seen in less important spheres than those of politics and war. It is perhaps especially visible in criticism. Let but some awful Aristarch speak out loud and bold, and the rest of the flock follow like sheep, turning each one in the way of the bell-wether. The statement may be contrary to demonstrable fact—it makes no difference. It is a dogma, and must be believed on pain of exclusion from the literary heaven. So-and-so has said it three times; it is therefore obviously true. One could adduce a score of recent instances; but it is better to refrain, lest an initial prejudice be created in the mind of the reader. It may, however, be safe to mention the dogma of the impeccability of Shakespeare—a dogma associated with the Athanasian names of Coleridge, Schlegel, and Victor Hugo. For more than half a century this creed held its ground, and it was not till quite recently that a few courageous spirits ventured to hint a fault and hesitate dislike of a passage here and there. Only very timidly has a more sober and rational view obtained a hearing. This instance is sufficient to show the evil of too easy an acceptance of mere authority.

Another example, as I hope to show, is provided by the dominant creed as to the style of Joseph Conrad—a writer of undoubted genius, whom it is far from the purpose of this paper to depreciate. But the common statement that Conrad writes English like an Englishman, and that it is impossible from his writings to detect his foreign birth, is simply false. He writes the language, it is true, with amazing vigour, and his vocabulary is both choice and enormous. But his style shows so many marks indicating that he thought in one language and wrote in another, as to make us wonder whether the critics in question can have read the books with any care. As a matter of fact, in this one respect—I am not at the moment speaking of any other—Maarten Maartens stands on a higher plane: the Dutchman's English, though less varied and abundant, and far less vigorously descriptive, is more native, and has fewer touches betraying the foreigner, than that of the Pole.

The fact is, that to write to perfection in more than one language is practically impossible. Gibbon, it is said, wrote French like Beaumarchais; but dull indeed is he who does not see plenty of Gallicisms in the *Decline and Fall*. What Italian fails to detect Anglicisms in the Italian sonnets of Milton? Bentham's French was remarkably good; none can say the same of his English. It is no blame then to Conrad if, every now and then, in the midst of passages glowing with eloquence, there peep out turns of phrase which, like a failure of accent in a speaker, point to his place of birth. If Gladstone was a Lancastrian to the day of his death, small wonder if Conrad remained a Slav. What *is* surprising is that judges of repute should have failed to see it, or, seeing, should have conspired to conceal it.

I have not, I repeat, the smallest wish to deny Conrad's genius. To criticise Pope's Homer is not to censure the *Odyssey*; and the true greatness of Conrad is not of a kind to be marred by a few defects in the medium he chose to employ. His penetration, his descriptive gift, his power of suggesting atmosphere, his equally extraordinary power of marshalling his episodes so as to lend decisive force to the final catastrophe, all these remain entirely unaffected by the fact that his writing is really translation. But one would be a poor eulogist who could not note faults; and a refusal to note faults is ultimately to do a disservice to the idol. As Lowell said to the critics who ranked *Thanatopsis* with *Tintern Abbey*:

> He's a very good Bryant,
> But, my friends, you'll endanger the life of your client
> By trying to stretch him out into a giant.

I propose, then, to illustrate my point by considering a long passage from one of Conrad's latest and best-known novels, and examining how far it deserves this particular praise. I choose a *continuous* passage, because it is in the number and frequency of certain kinds of flaw that the foreigner is shown. Our language is too difficult and elusive for even the native, however able and cautious, invariably to write it with correctness. There are errors not only in the looser authors, but also in the most exact: a few in Macaulay, many in Thackeray, many in Ruskin, and multitudes in Froude. But, first, these are *English* errors; they are the mistakes which the Englishman makes, and are in harmony with the spirit of the language. And, secondly, they occur at random intervals, more or less frequently according to the accuracy or carelessness, the freshness or fatigue, of the writer. The mistakes of Conrad are not those of a native (except in so far as he had picked up inaccuracies from his models), nor are they in harmony with our stylistic habits; while they occur again and again, in exactly the places where we should expect them to occur. Often they are what we may imagine the Greek of a Jebb or the

Latin of a Munro to be—not precisely incorrect, breaking no rule, and yet putting things in a way in which no ancient Greek or Roman would ever put them. We must all have seen compositions by foreigners, in which no syntactical law is violated, and for every phrase in which, perhaps, authority might be found, yet which have a quite unmistakably alien air. At times the foreigner is bewrayed, in writing as so often in conversation, by an excess of accuracy. He is afraid to play with his new language as he can play with his own. So it is with much of Conrad. It is quite possible, to take an example, that he has fewer laxities than an author like Washington Irving. But no one reading Irving can doubt for a moment that he is writing in his mother-tongue. Not so with Conrad. Nor, indeed, does he by any means always avoid definite solecisms. And, having learned his English mainly from talk, he was not always alive to the difference between the colloquial style and the style of prose. We are thus, occasionally, in the middle of a soaring flight, brought suddenly down to earth.

I ask, therefore, the attention of my readers while I run through with them the first three or four chapters of *The Rover*. I am quite conscious that this choice is to some extent unduly favourable to my purpose; for the exotic character of the style is here more than usually manifest; so manifest indeed that I have sometimes fancied these chapters to have

been written early in Conrad's career, before practice had given him the degree of mastery which he
attained later. To hazard a guess, I fancy he may
well have thrown them aside, as Scott threw *Waver-
ley*, and resumed them several years later: a certain
unevenness in the book, as in Scott's, would thus be
accounted for. But the choice is made in order that
my readers, by keeping the book open before them,
may be able without difficulty to follow my obser-
vations, and if necessary correct my judgments. For
the same reason I take as they come the passages on
which I wish to dwell, and do not arrange the errors
under heads. This method may appear haphazard,
and certainly has its disadvantages; but I believe the
disadvantages to be on the whole outweighed by
the conveniences. I quote from the edition of 1923.

(1) p. 7. But as to that, old Peyrol had made up his mind
from the first to blow up his valuable charge—unemotionally,
for such was his character, formed under the sun of the
Indian seas in lawless contests with his kind for a little loot
that vanished as soon as grasped, but mainly for bare life
almost as precarious to hold through its ups and downs, and
which now had lasted for fifty-eight years.

Here is a sentence which assuredly would never have
been written by any Englishman since the seventeenth
century. In it are summed up very many of the
characteristic faults which we shall notice repeatedly
as we proceed. First, there is the trick of placing the
adverb in an awkwardly detached position. It is

Conrad's habit to put it after the verb in cases when a natural English would put it before; and here the habit has a specially bad result, for we are not sure at first sight whether the word *unemotionally* is to be taken with *made up his mind* or with *blow up his charge*. With *formed under the sun* we light on another Conradian peculiarity, of which we shall have many examples: that of adding to a sentence already finished a long adjectival *phrase*. An Englishman, even if he gave way to such a habit, would generally use an adjectival *clause* introduced by a relative; but, as we shall notice, Conrad dislikes relative clauses. *Grasped*, again, is strange. We often say "He came when called"; but rarely do we use *as soon as* without a verb. It is more natural for us to say "Come as soon as *you are* ready" than to say "Come as soon as ready"; and it is exceedingly clumsy to use such a phrase when the final word is not an adjective but a participle. *And which* in the last line is inaccurate, for there is no previous *which* to justify the *and*. *Almost as precarious to hold* is another adjectival *phrase*, most inartistically hung on to the word *life*. Whether *through its ups and downs* is an adverb of cause, or goes closely with *hold*, is left uncertain. Finally, the sentence as a whole is a typically bad example of the worst form of the "period"—that in which, after the main clause has been passed, a number of subordinate clauses are dragged in. One is quite breathless long before the end; and there is nothing but the full stop to show that the end has been reached.

(2) p. 8. While his crew swarmed aloft...to furl the sails nearly as thin and as patched as the grimy shirts on their backs, Peyrol took a survey of the quay.

Here once more we have the long phrase-adjective, hanging almost as uneasily on *the sails* as the least skilled of the crew on the yards. What adds to the annoyance of the reader is the detestable system of no-punctuation adopted by the printers; and yet, so bad is the sentence that, if a comma *were* inserted between *sails* and *nearly*, we should naturally think it was the crew, and not the sails, that were thin and patched.

(3) p. 8. He shaved his big cheeks with a real English razor, looted years ago from an officer's cabin in an English East Indiaman, captured by a ship he was serving in then.

Ago is incorrect; it is not surprising that a foreigner should not be able to distinguish it from *before*. *Then*, though without emphasis, is placed in an unusual and therefore emphatic position. *Captured*, coming in this way subordinately after *looted*, drags the sentence, and seems to forebode a series of participles as long as the series of relatives in *The House that Jack built*.

(4) p. 9. He did not get rid of his followers till the door of the Port Office.

What Englishman ever misused the word *till* in this fashion?

(5) p. 9. Looking everybody coldly in the eye.

A phrase which occurs again—p. 11. Though it is not uncommon, *in the face* would be more natural.

(6) p. 10. In the various offices connected with the sea where his duties took him.

Note *connected* for future use. Who would not think that *where* referred to *sea?* And, in any case, would not a native writer say either *whither* or *to which?*

(7) p. 11. His large face of the Roman type.

More naturally, "His large face, with its Roman features."

But a really good writer would have described the face beforehand, and contented himself with the merest allusion to its peculiarities when he came to refer to it later. Conrad was misled by the tricks of the word *of,* which are different in every language from what they are in every other. We can say "Her box of chocolates attracted attention," but hardly "Her box of a strange shape attracted attention": common as such a phrase is in French, and (I imagine) in Polish also[1].

(8) p. 12. Nobody could know...unless he told *them.*

This laxity, which is common enough in talk, is due, like the similar *they* on p. 13, line 9 (Every...they), to the colloquial origin of Conrad's English.

---

[1] Readers of Arnold Bennett will have observed how, in his later novels, he affects this French idiom.

(9) p. 13. Far away...there was the sea of the Hyères roadstead with a lumpy indigo swelling still beyond.

It turns out that *swelling* is a noun, and that *still beyond* means *still further out*.

(10) p. 13. Of himself running barefooted in connection with a flock of turkeys, with hardly any clothes on his back.

In connection with, which is a favourite phrase of Conrad's, can rarely have been used more strangely than here: and a good writer would assuredly have put the last seven words immediately after *barefooted*.

(11) p. 15. The name of the farmer Peyrol attached to his person on account of his inability to give a clear account of himself acquired a sort of reputation, both openly, in the ports of the East, and secretly amongst the Brothers of the Coast, that strange fraternity with something masonic and not a little piratical in its constitution.

A typical Conrad sentence. Note first the long adjective beginning with *attached*. A native writer would certainly have said something like this: The name of the farmer Peyrol, which our hero, on account of his inability to give a clear account of himself, assumed....

But so obscure is the sentence that no one can say with any assurance whether *attached* is really a participle after all, or whether it is a past tense with a relative omitted ("the name of the farmer, *which* Peyrol attached to his person"); and when we have solved that insoluble question we have still to face a whole crowd of subordinate clauses and phrases tacked on anyhow to any word that may turn up. No rule is sounder than that, in a long periodic sentence, the subordinate parts should be so arranged that we cannot imagine the sentence to be finished before it actually *does* conclude; and no rule is more frequently violated by Conrad. Such a violation recurs on the very next page:

(12) He felt a little funny as it were, and the funniest thing was the thought which crossed his mind that he could indulge his fancy (if he had a mind to do it) to buy up all this land to the furthermost field, away over there where the track lost itself sinking into the flats bordering the sea where the small rise at the end of the Giens peninsula had assumed the appearance of a black cloud.

Not to mark the colloquialisms, we may ask why this sentence should ever have ended.

(13) p. 16. If I had stayed in this country I would be talking like this fellow.

It is not surprising that Conrad, mixing with Scotsmen, Americans, and Irishmen, should have failed to master our idiomatic use of *should* and *would*: and, after noticing this one example, I shall say nothing of the hundreds of others which might be adduced.

(14) p. 18. He had been wearing next his bare skin—like a pious penitent his hair-shirt—a sort of waistcoat made of two thicknesses of old sailcloth and stitched all over in the manner of a quilt with tarred twine.

On this sentence there is no need to comment: it is

well illustrated by one that occurs only ten lines below:

(15) Peyrol drew a long breath into his broad chest with a pepper and salt pelt down the breastbone.

A truly remarkable way of breathing! We recommend it to those who may be called upon to apply artificial respiration.

(16) p. 19. He did not want to own any part of the solid earth for which he had no love.

Again ambiguous: an ordinary reader would take the antecedent of *which* to be *any part*; thus taken the sentence is tautologous nonsense. Read: "He had no love for the solid earth, and did not want to own any part of it." Passing over a dozen other exotic sentences to be found by the curious reader in the next two or three pages—there are indeed scarcely five consecutive lines in which an adverb or an adjective does not appear in a wrong place—we come to:

(17) p. 22. With that gravity from which he seldom departed he inquired if there were any inhabitants besides himself in the village.

Here one's first impression is that Peyrol is the *himself*: but as he has only just arrived in the village he can hardly be included among the inhabitants. What is meant is that he asks of a man he has met whether there are any inhabitants in addition to *that man*: Conrad is trying to put into *oratio obliqua* Peyrol's question, "Is there anybody living here besides yourself?"; and a terrible mess he makes of his task.

(18) p. 23. "I have a sort of hut down by the lagoon..." the man confessed, as it were.

As it were, which is a common cliché of Conrad's (see 12 above), is a sad trap for the unwary; but there are few English writers who would use it in this manner, as if with the set purpose of making the sentence end in the flattest way conceivable. Either omit it or read: "The man answered, and his answer was as it were a confession."

(19) p. 25. You don't look like anything that has been seen here for years.... You look like one, I dare hardly say what.

Here it is plain that Polish, like so many other languages, does not distinguish between *a* and *one*. What Conrad means is, "You look like a—I daren't say what": and this single sentence is sufficient to show his origin; for it is one that not the most ignorant Englishman that ever lived could possibly have written.

(20) p. 30. But Peyrol knew how to be patient, with that patience that is so often a form of courage. He was known for it. It had served him well in dangerous situations. Once it had saved his life. Nothing but patience. He could well wait now. He waited.

The relative *that* should be *which*; and the short sentences are unparalleled even in Macaulay. One effect of the shortness is that the sentence "Nothing but patience" is ambiguous: it really means that mere patience had saved his life; but it might well be taken to mean that nothing but patience was required in that particular emergency.

These examples may seem more than sufficient; but it will perhaps be not out of place to give a few more, with or without comment:

(21) p. 33. He had adapted himself, by means of passive acquiescence, to the new and inexplicable conditions of life in something like twenty-four hours.

(22) p. 36. He was rewarded for his self-restraint and the unshaken good-humour with which he had conducted the discussion by carrying his point.

(23) p. 38. The vast semicircle of barren high hills, broken by the entrance to Toulon harbour guarded by forts and batteries.

(24) p. 42. Without ever being led astray by the nature, or the cruelty, or the danger of any given situation [nature *includes* the cruelty and the danger][1].

(25) p. 44. His head with a Roman profile propped up on a mighty and tattooed forearm [the profile propped up].

(26) p. 45. Peyrol...opened his big sandalwood chest secured with an enormous padlock.

(27) p. 48. That sea rover turned rustic was now perfectly at home in that farm which, like a lighthouse, commanded the view of two roadsteads and the open sea.

Here we light on a trick of phrase which is exceed-

---

[1] I do not add (p. 42) "This won't prevent *me* sleeping" for "prevent *my* sleeping" or "*me* from": for bad *English* writers often make the same mistake: nor do I notice (p. 43) "an artificiality *of which* he had never heard and would have appeared puzzling": though good English demands *which* before *would*.

ingly common in French, but very rare in English: the trick of trying to sum up in a subordinate clause a great deal of information which we English should give independently. (No. 7 above is an example.) We may often notice in French a mention (say) of Hannibal immediately followed by a sentence like this: "This great heroic general, insensible alike to the extremes of heat and of cold, the idol of the soldiers, and of the same age as Napoleon when he invaded Italy, who took[1] poison at sixty-three to escape capture, half-god, half-demon, determined to assail Saguntum." A bad French writer often introduces into this front clause a whole set of statements utterly irrelevant in the context; a good one attends to appropriateness; but bad and good alike are alien to the English spirit, which would give a character of Hannibal in separate sentences, and then proceed, "With this equipment, the young general began his task." There is no irrelevance in this particular sentence of Conrad's; but the trick betrays him; and even without the trick, we should know him by the *that* at the beginning.

(28) p. 49. A young man greeted him *by* a careless nod.

Prepositions are the most idiomatic parts of every speech; and you will find Germans, after twenty years in England, saying they have come *with* the train.

---

[1] French, in which *et qui* is idiomatic, would probably say "et qui but."

(29) p. 50. The slamming of the salle door broke the silence between the two gazers on the sea.

Here again an attempt *to work things in.* Either "the two sea-gazers," or "They gazed long in silence at the sea. The silence was broken. ..."

At about this point the style becomes noticeably more English; and it is hereabouts that I suspect Conrad of having thrown the novel aside, to resume it when he had acquired a closer acquaintance with his medium. Not that the errors, though fewer, are entirely absent. We find, for instance, on p. 97:

(30) A phenomenon and a wonder to the natives, as it had happened to him before on more than one island in distant seas.

The solecistic use of *phenomenon* is undoubtedly a too common native mistake; but the peculiar use of *as it had happened* is Conrad's own.

On p. 110 are several treacherous phrases, of which, to conclude our strictures, we may select three or four:

(31) This, on his part, was a simple delusion.

No Englishman would ever use *on his part*, at least in this position, in such a manner.

(32) Contemplated him with his brown eyes, which had an upward cast naturally.

The late and therefore emphatic position of *naturally* gives the sentence a meaning totally unintended.

(33) His companion completed his significant silence, which seemed to have been occupied with thoughts very like his own, by saying....

Completed, like *his* and *his own*, is ambiguous; it may mean either *filled up* or *ended*, but in either case it is the wrong word.

(34) He spent *a lot* of his time on board.

Too colloquial for the style of the context.

There may be a difference of opinion as to some of my statements; but when every deduction has been made, it will remain a wonder how any critic, knowing his own language, can possibly have given Conrad's prose the particular praise which it has so often received. And, be it remembered, that, however many of my examples be ruled out, it would be easy to find a dozen others to claim the place of every one rejected. The result of all this is that Conrad is one of the very hardest of writers to read. Almost every other sentence requires close attention if its true meaning is to be unravelled; and the student (I use the word advisedly) is almost as weary after ten or twenty pages of him as if they were pages of Greek. I do not deny that it is possible to find, here and there, in the writings of Englishmen, sentences as confused as many of his. This from Evelyn's *Diary*, for example, is quite Conradian:

Thus died King Charles II of a vigorous and robust constitution, and in all appearance promising a long life (*Diary*, Feb. 6, 1685);

but what is permissible in a private journal is inexcusable in books meant for publication. And I do not deny that there are many merits in Conrad which make it fully worth the while of the student to face the labour of reading him. But to pretend that these confusions and difficulties do not exist is merely exasperating: it is like those official denials of what everybody knows to be true, which convince nobody and merely increase the general distrust of officials. We cannot hope to get rid of these from politics; but they ought to be rigidly banished from the realm of criticism.

xiii

Of Faerie lond yet if he more inquyre,
By certaine signs, here set in sondrie place,
He may it fynd.
                    SPENSER, *F.Q.* II. Proem.

THE greatest difficulty in the way of confident
and sound criticism is the constant shifting in the
standards of taste. Every critic, however cautious
or independent, is necessarily the child of his age
and of his nationality, and has no guarantee that
before long some revolution in men's attitude may
not put all his views out of date and render all his
judgments nugatory. As modes alter in the realm
of dress, nay, even in physical beauty, so the fashion
alters in the realm of literature, and that which was
once admired is cast aside in favour of something
new, or, not infrequently, in favour of that which
was once despised. Forty or fifty years ago, for
example, red hair was almost literally the "head
and front" of ugliness, and the source of misery to
its possessor: a Burne-Jones arose, and red hair
became beautiful and fashionable. But Burne-Jones
was only re-introducing an earlier type; in the days
of Shakespeare "black was the badge of hell, the
hue of demons," and Queen Elizabeth disguised her
natural tresses under a false red. In the time of
Dante, if we may judge by his eulogies of Beatrice

and her "occhi smaragdi," green eyes were beautiful; they have certainly not always been so. And similarly, in the time of Johnson, Gothic architecture was the chosen symbol of barbarism, ready to everybody's hand, and Gray was regarded as eccentric for praising the cathedrals of Chartres and Amiens. The case of Wagner illustrates the same thing in the sphere of music. That sound musician, John Hullah, was found playing Wagner upside down, as the only way to make sense of him. He had tried him forwards and backwards, and failed to detect any harmony. Within a few years Wagner ranked with Beethoven, and within a few more there were many to vote him a "back number."

In poetry we find, perhaps still more often, a like phenomenon. A Cowley takes the world by storm: a generation passes, and Pope asks, "Who now reads Cowley?" Pope himself becomes the *ne plus ultra* of genius, and the *Essay on Man* is the height of the sublime. Half a century after his death it is seriously debated whether he is a poet at all. Byron's *Cain*, said Scott in 1821, "certainly matches Milton on his own ground"; in 1860 people did not stop to consider such a judgment; they smiled at it and passed on. Edgar Allan Poe expressed the deliberate opinion that Tennyson was the greatest poet that ever lived: where is Tennyson now? But this is far from all. There has been, in almost every case, a reaction against the reaction; Pope and Byron are already more or less restored to favour, and there is every sign that the restoration of Tennyson will not be long delayed. Nor may the restoration, in its turn, be final; if we may judge the future by the past, there will yet be many ebbs and flows of opinion.

Facts like these have led certain philosophers to adopt the view that there is no such thing as absolute beauty at all. Lord Balfour, to take but one instance, carries his scepticism to an extreme point, and holds that the Hottentot Venus is lovely to the Hottentot and Aphrodite to the Greek; both judgments being merely relative, and one goddess no more beautiful, in the absolute sense, than the other. Unlike Burke, who amid all differences contrived to maintain that there is the same standard of taste, somehow, in all men, Lord Balfour declares that no such standard exists, or—what is the same thing— that there are innumerable such standards. Beauty is what pleases; and, as it is indubitable that different things please different men, and the same men at different times, beauty is a variable entity, blown about by every wind of doctrine.

Be this as it may, there is no doubt that an absolute standard is very hard to attain, and that, if it could be attained, men would differ in the way they applied it to individual works of art. Assume, for the sake of argument, that we have one canon; our methods of measuring by it would still vary from man to man. We might all agree that a certain work has *some* beauty; we should never agree as to how far it falls short of the "great idea" to which it ought to correspond: and the failure would be appraised by some as almost negligible, by others as important.

What, then, in the face of all these shiftings of standard, is the critic to do? Nothing, it would seem, is more certain than that whatever he says, if read at all in the future, will be ridiculed as absurd, or at best be wondered at as paradoxical. Even while he is writing, the change may be taking place, and his views may be antiquated as soon as they are published. As he reflects that this work, which seems to him flamboyant or overstrained, may be the pioneer of a new school of writing, that this other, which he conscientiously admires, may be doomed to early damnation, must he—as is so often done by timid reviewers—carefully "hedge" in every expression of opinion, and leave a loophole of escape from every apparently decisive statement? Must he, like a politician faced with a ticklish situation, take refuge in guarded ambiguities, or, as Newman would have put it, steer clear of Scylla and Charybdis through the channel of No-meaning? Or is he to risk the fate of a Jeffrey when confronted with a new *Excursion*, and boldly say "This will never do" —heedless of the chance that posterity may find that it "does" very well?

Fortunately, there is one foundation that stands sure amid the trembling sands—and that is, plain and simple straightforwardness. Every man to whom the duty of expressing an opinion falls, must express it honestly without fear or favour. Nothing, even in the future, is gained by timidity, disguise, or equivocation: it is better to be an upright Jeffrey, with all his blindness, rejecting a Wordsworth and welcoming a Mr Barrett, than one who, for fear of being found wanting later, dodges and palters with his own convictions. Better be the man who says openly that he hates Hardy and admires Marie Corelli, than the man who, like some critics that might be named, waits to see what others will say before he speaks out himself. All honest, though mistaken, criticism has its value: it reveals at least *one* man. Nay, to some extent it reveals two. After all, the merit of a book, like that of a speech, depends on two parties, the author and the reader, and we can know little of a book till we know its effect on the latter. A written book is nothing until it is read, as the external world is nothing without a perceiver: and the worth of a book is merely the sum of the impressions it makes on *all* its readers. The stupidest and most uninformed opinion is some part of that total worth; and it is therefore desirable that even that stupid and uninformed opinion should be fearlessly expressed. A book of permanent value is one of which the averaged judgment of all its readers is on the whole favourable: the *Excursion* would have had a still greater value than it has if it had pleased not only later ages but contemporaries; precisely as the speeches of Burke would have been still better than they are if they had been approved by their hearers as well as by us readers. A writer unpopular in his own day has lost *something*; and a writer who pleases a considerable number of his contemporaries must have *some* merit. And the criticism which registers this pleasure has its worth also. We are apt to laugh, like Milton's Deity, at the "quaint opinions wide" of our predecessors; we ought to be grateful to them for showing to us a very important part of the character of the work they seem to us to have appraised so feebly: whereas neutral and non-committal judgments but tell us what we knew before, that every age has its Mr Facing-both-ways and Mr Two-tongues, trying to make the best of both worlds.

At the same time, an honest opinion, erroneous or otherwise, need not be careless or uninstructed. Though there be no attainable and unalterable criterion of beauty, and though few things are more precarious than the ascription of any great measure of beauty to a work of art, yet there are sundry marks, of a relatively absolute kind, for which the critic can look out, and which, as far as they go, are all but infallible indications of merit: some of them, indeed, are so precise and definite as to be well-nigh removed from the shadowy world of taste, and to fall under the more rigid sway of mathematics. As in law there is no means by which an innocent man can be always certain of acquittal, while yet there are definite rules by which a miscarriage of justice is rendered unlikely, so in literary criticism, while we can never be free from the *possibility* of condemning the good books or praising the bad, yet there are some principles, less of taste than of common sense, which if carefully borne in mind may make such errors as rare as, we trust, those of judge and jury are in another court. They are, in fact, such that, if steadily applied, no court of appeal, though it may reverse the verdict, can justly convict us of *crassa ignorantia.*

Mr Lascelles Abercrombie, in a very able book, has attempted to apply some such principles with the object of distinguishing, once for all, between "great" poetry and what is merely "good." There is much that is suggestive, as well as something that is doubtful, in his essay; but our present purpose is not quite the same as his, and we are therefore free from the necessity of discussing his views. What we are trying to discover is not the criteria by which we can draw the boundary between two classes of good literature, but marks incontrovertible and—a modicum of care and intelligence being assumed—unmistakable, which will at the least secure us against grosser critical errors; which will, for example, prevent us from taking the *Epic of Hades* for a new *Inferno,* or *Cato* for a new *Julius Caesar*: and, on the other hand, save us from the far worse error of throwing aside a *Tintern Abbey*. This is a humble aim, but it is at any rate a useful one; and, as such mistakes have been made, it is a necessary one. And, in my opinion, it may be more or less completely attained.

The first of these marks is symmetry of design —architectonic harmony: the sort of proportion which, in its measure, is to be found in Gray's poems, and which ought to have prevented Dr Johnson from perpetrating his unfavourable criticism. A reviewer, for example, presented with *Paradise Lost* for the first time, might possibly be perplexed about the language, which would be strange, or about the philosophy, which is open to argument. Certain individual passages, also, here and there, might trouble him, and he might even, like many eighteenth-century readers, boggle at the blank verse. But no one not hopelessly prejudiced, if he has eyes to see, can have any doubt about the structural completeness of the scheme, the perfection of which is as obvious as that of Giotto's circle. No better-rounded whole was ever given to the world. The reader may not like the scheme in itself; but that it is worked out with almost perfect balance and proportion cannot be denied. *So far*, then, the verdict is unavoidable; *Paradise Lost* is a great poem: and, incidentally, the fact that this symmetry was achieved by a blind man, without the help of visible notes or scenario, makes the work, from this point of view alone, one of the most astounding feats of human genius. Much the same can be said of the *Divine Comedy*, some of the details in which may be censured, but which as a finished whole is beyond praise. On the same level, in this aspect, stands *Othello*. With slight reservations, a critic set down before *Tom Jones* would be compelled, by sheer mathematics, and despite all possible vagaries of *taste*, to pass a similar judgment. All these, and others that might be named, have, as Aristotle would have put it, a beginning, a middle, and an end.

Thus, then, when the critic lights on a new work, if he finds in it some approach to the architectonic power shown in these immortal achievements, he is on sure ground. To that extent the work is good, and, if posterity does not think so, the worse for posterity, which will assuredly be corrected by a posterity of its own. For it must be remembered that the generation least likely to be right is the one just following an author. The first reaction in criticism, as in everything else, is the most violent; and the generation which has heard its parents praising too profusely is almost certain to go too far in dispraise. Thus, for instance, the present-day view of Tennyson is the most likely to be proved wrong by the considered judgment of the ages. A young man, tired of hearing Aristides called the Just, takes the first opportunity of ostracising him; but it does not follow that his opinion is any more trustworthy than that of those who have known Aristides from his youth up; nor is the opinion of the Georgian generation on Tennyson an unassailable one.

The second mark is truth to humanity; and by this I mean truth to those great and deep-seated elements in human nature which seem to have been proved by time to be permanent and basal; all but independent of circumstance; liable perhaps to be disturbed occasionally, but always reasserting themselves when the disturbing cause has been removed; the "eternal" principles of justice, veracity, purity; the emotions of indignation at wrong, of admiration for courage, of pity for undeserved misfortune. Such is the truth of the *Iliad*; we to-day feel, as the contemporaries of Homer felt, indignation at the treatment of Achilles, pity for Priam and Andromache, sympathy with the devotion of Patroclus and Hector, a glow of enthusiasm for bravery, a scorn of cowardice. All these are elemental emotions, stamped with the mark of permanence by their essential rightness. It is this truth to real human nature which we see in the seventh book of Thucydides; we are overcome, and our descendants to the twentieth generation will be overcome, by the tale of catastrophe, by the tragedy of Nicias, by the "tears of things." And, conversely, when we see writers making much of passing and accidental emotions, of dislocations of morality caused by abnormal events, of a state of affairs which obviously belongs to a period of transition; when we see them confounding the momentary with the eternal, and the parochial with the universal, then we may be sure that the success, however dazzling it may be, will be ephemeral. Here we have a test by which we may appraise the multitude of "problem" novels which have crowded our libraries during the last few years. As it is certain that a country which should adopt the "system" of morality preached in these books, and keep it up for any considerable time, would dissolve into chaos, so it is certain that these novels can have no lasting value. We have but one choice. Either these novels must cease to speak the real voice of the country—in which case they will be forgotten; or the country will adopt their principles and perish—and the novels with it. They will be studied, if at all, as the documents of the decaying Roman Empire are studied, by scholars intent on discovering the predisposing causes of the ruin.

Thirdly, we look out for a certain accuracy and precision in the author's use of language, a certain selection, a reliance on the sound and proved elements of the English tongue. The slangy, the specialised, the technical, the precious, are signs of the transitory. Defects of grammar, when carried beyond reasonable limits, again, betoken a want of clearness in the mind. Not, of course, that we must expect absolute perfection; the English language is as full of snares as the Vale of Siddim was full of slime-pits, and we must allow for an occasional stumble. But there are certain errors into which no good writer falls, and others into which he falls but rarely; whereas the bad writer falls into both with revealing frequency. In a not unsuccessful novel of recent years, of three hundred not too closely printed pages, were counted more than two hundred solecisms: and in a very popular one by an author recently dead there are eighty or ninety examples of a single class of mistake, the confusion of *who* and *whom*. It is safe to say that neither of these writers can survive.

With regard to vocabulary, care is specially necessary; for not even taste changes more quickly than the atmosphere of words. What, for instance, was the poetical dialect of the eighteenth century is to-day the prosiest of mediums: and what seems to us good and appropriate language may in a few years, through no fault of ours, acquire unsuitable associations. It is no blame to Pope that "clasped the blooming hero in her arms" is now ridiculous; and when Matthew Arnold censured Gray for "Thy joys no glittering female meets," he was really blaming not Gray but the changes in language. A little thought would have shown him that, if such an artist as Gray used the word "female," it was because "female" was then a dignified and poetical word. There will certainly be Arnolds in the future to censure *our* dialect, because to *them* it will have unlucky associations.

Still, there are elements in the English tongue which can scarcely be degraded, and an author who uses it as Goldsmith or Swift used it can hardly ever become really old-fashioned. At any rate, the absence of cant, the avoidance of meaningless expressions, the rarity of tags and clichés, will be obvious amid all the changes, as such merits are plain to us in the dialogues of Plato or the speeches of Demosthenes; and these merits are not matters of mere taste, but can be reckoned almost as passionlessly as a set of statistics.

The late Richard Moulton, perplexed, like everybody else, by the vagaries of criticism, proposed what he called an "inductive" principle; that is, he desired to give up all *a priori* rules, and to base his judgments on established facts. Those writings which have survived the storms of many generations, or which (to change the metaphor) have borne translation from one climate to another, are to be assumed, in virtue of this universal appeal, to have in themselves some quality of absolute beauty. From these, Moulton argued, our canons are to be drawn; these, at any rate, are the writings that *have* survived, and by comparison with them we must decide what writings *will* survive.

There is plainly one objection to this theory, if there are no more. It does not follow, because certain books have survived, that the qualities they possess are the only ones that ensure survival. To argue thus is to commit the old logical fallacy of simple conversion; to say that because Englishmen are Europeans, Europeans are Englishmen. There may be innumerable characteristics, not seen in the *Iliad* or in *Macbeth*, which a book may possess, and which may turn out to be marks of the great and permanent. No two works can easily differ more widely than the *Pilgrim's Progress* and *Tristram Shandy*; and yet, if it is safe to prophesy on anything at all, it is safe to prophesy that both will be immortal. A new genre, different from either, may at any moment be evolved by a man of genius. Again, it cannot be too strongly emphasised that permanence is not by itself a proof of merit. All sorts of accidental influences may keep a book alive, or at least may drag it from its grave at short intervals. The *In Ctesiphontem* of Aeschines is not a very great speech; but it will live or vegetate by its relation to the immortal discourse to which it gave birth. The Augustan histories, again, are actually bad books; but they are first-hand authorities on a period which can never lose its interest. The *Satires* of Persius (*pace* Casaubon and Conington) might almost be used as a handbook of faults to be avoided; but they attract notice, and will continue to attract notice, for the light they throw on the times and on the Stoic philosophy. Certain old English and French books might be mentioned which have nothing to recommend them except the fact that they *are* old; a recommendation which they will obviously continue to have in increasing measure. Thus we must apply Moulton's canon with caution. Still, if carefully guarded it has its use. We must not at once rule out the new because it differs from the old; but we may pretty safely rule in the new when it resembles the old. We must not reject Wordsworth because he is unlike Pope; but if we light on a work with Pope's energy, brevity, and liveliness, we may safely add that work to our library of classics. I would not be misunderstood. A large part of the greatness of the old consists in their originality; and a mere imitation of it differs from it in precisely the most important respect. But if the new writer—to quote words that can scarcely be bettered—wears the garb but not the clothes of the ancients, if he shows qualities which will pass the severe ordeal of comparison with them, then his works will probably last as long as theirs have lasted, while those which will not pass the ordeal will probably die. The absence, then, of eccentricity, violence, paradox, exaggeration, an absence conspicuous in the vast majority of the greatest works, is our fourth mark of lasting merit, as the presence of far-fetched conceits, of overstrain, of forcible-feebleness, is a symptom of a disease that will probably bring about an early death. Such a rule, it is only too clear, will exclude many books of to-day which have achieved a considerable vogue.

All these features are to be found in the Silver Ages of literatures that have been tottering to their dissolution: but they have assuredly never been more common than now. Never were more passions torn to tatters, never did writers contort themselves more violently in their desire to gain notoriety than they do to-day. The noisy, the grotesque, the startling, win a hearing, win an audience, and have their reward; but the still small voice carries the true message. The great old writers knew what they had to say, and said it, directly and simply. The moderns shout in the market-places, and soon wear out their own throats and the patience of their hearers. While then a critic will not fail to recognise that a man who pleases his contemporaries must have *some* worth, he will easily detect in such as these the signs which the soothsayer saw in Charles I: a crowd may cheer him, but his day will be short.

Lastly, a writer who, whatever be his beauty of language, is shallow in thought, and destitute of that indefinable something known as personality, will deservedly die. It does not follow that those who have these marks will live; for many of them deliberately write, as statesmen speak, with an eye to their own age, and some of the profoundest works ever written have been tentative and expect to be superseded—nay, themselves provide the material for their own supersession. They belong to what De Quincey called the "literature of knowledge," and often, of set purpose, avoid the sphere of "power": what they teach is but as seed sown that in due time quickens into other forms. But the true "literature of power" must none the less reveal a mind greater and more comprehensive than the book itself: the reader must instinctively feel that he is in the presence of a commanding intellect. Whether he dislikes that intellect or not is of no importance; his very dislike may be a tribute to its greatness—as Calverley's furious attack upon Browning showed how high he felt Browning to be. He would not have wasted all that frenzy on something he really felt to be contemptible. But when the book is obviously trying to make its author seem greater than itself, it is a sham, and may be rejected. Much of Swinburne, for example, is dead already, because he went on talking and gesticulating when, for the time being, he had little to say. Now this "message," this impact of mind on mind, cannot be mistaken by a trained intelligence, and shows itself through all impediments. And that though it expresses itself in style. It has been truly said that the best elements of style are those that do not vanish when the book passes into another tongue: and it is these elements that will keep a book alive when it passes into the foreign tongue of our descendants. Chaucer, to take one instance, is partially strange to us, and Cynewulf well-nigh as far removed as Homer. Yet their style, in this highest sense, still appeals, and we can tell the difference between *Troilus* and the *Confessio Amantis*. Who, though but a beginner in Greek, does not feel the grandeur of Aeschylus or the limpidity of Plato? We lose much by not being contemporaries and countrymen of the author of *Job*; but his greatness, and his greatness of *style*, is still visible, because the sublimity of his mind and thought cannot be obscured by a strange idiom. We know Isaiah, though we cannot read his language, and though the best Hebrew scholars are often at a loss as to his exact meaning. Style, after all, is the man; and the great man can always be recognised, immediately and almost infallibly. Where there is a dominating personality behind the book, we can see it. What is wanting to-day, when all is said, is less the ability to write than the ability to *be*. Where that is present, a permanent influence, overt or secret, is assured.

And so of the critic himself. When we study the judgments of the past, we observe that those which have failed to stand the test of time usually reveal a certain weakness, intellectual or moral, in the critic, sometimes it is true pardonable and inevitable, sometimes blameworthy or avoidable. He has, it may be, failed to look at the work before him with his own eyes, and waited too much on the fashion of the time. Or he has allowed his judgment to be warped by prejudice, personal or political. Or—which is a very common crime—he has been too hasty in his perusal; a casual glance has been enough and he has appraised a book by its preface or by a few pages picked out here and there. Again, he has not considered the object and point of view of his author, and has therefore failed as completely to understand him as Job's friends failed to understand Job. Johnson criticising Milton, Dennis criticising Pope, had many merits, but it was not in them to approach their authors with detachment. Voltaire, writing nominally on Shakespeare, had his eye, in actual fact, on his own enemies in Paris. Others, again, were intent rather on glorifying themselves than on illuminating the work they were reviewing. And, even when all these distorting influences were absent, many were incapable of the *intellectual* exertion required to understand their author's scope and purpose. It was thus that the majority of eighteenth-century critics failed with Dante, Chaucer, and Shakespeare. But a critic like Dryden, open-minded, receptive, and liberal, could not really fail, and, despite all the disadvantages of inadequate knowledge, attained very nearly to the truth.

After all, then, we return to honesty as the essential. As, in Milton's phrase, he who aspires to be a poet must himself be a true poem, so he who aspires to be a critic must himself be a true man. Littleness, jealousy, prejudice, want of diligence, will never detect greatness. If we would appreciate rightly the work of others, we must first make our own calling and election sure.

For EU product safety concerns, contact us at Calle de José Abascal, 56–1°, 28003 Madrid, Spain or eugpsr@cambridge.org.